WES ANDERSON

SOPHIE MONKS KAUFMAN

WILLIAM
COLLINS

CONTENTS

INTRODUCTION

Family as the hand that feeds and bleeds you

Jack (Jason Schwartzman) aims a can of
mace at his brother Francis (Owen Wilson)
in the 2007 film *The Darjeeling Limited*. In
the process he distills a number of recurring truths
in the work of the Houston, Texas-born writer/
director Wes Anderson: families are hotbeds of
hurt; family members lie, disappoint and reject
one another, often at the most devastating of times;
and parents often fail to look after or even stay

alive for their children. The pain of coming from a dysfunctional home is writ large across every Anderson picture. And yet, for all the drama this pain causes, the subsequent hurt is rarely terminal. With reddened eyes and harbouring a lightly comic sense of stifled justice, the family unit limps on.

Children in adults' clothing

Unlike in happily-ever-after children's yarns, Wes Anderson's characters don't get what they initially think they want. Or else they do but only briefly, before time dispatches them onwards. This sounds bleak, and would be if presented in a stark manner. However Wes's films are the opposite of stark. He builds spectacles infused with childlike wonder, and in doing so sweetens the pill of certain death. If there is a message to be taken from all these images it is: don't be a jaded grown-up while there's still time on the clock. Wes almost sabotages himself by employing a childlike delivery of adult wisdom. Instead of having all the elements of cinema at the service of a single view, he has profound emotions dressed up in ornate doll's clothing in what is almost a tonal conflict.

The recurring fact of someone coming unglued

'I guess when I think about it, one of the things I like to dramatise, and what is sometimes funny, is someone coming unglued', said Anderson in a 2012 interview. We watch as his characters come unglued from life's big external mechanisms – work, the law, the Scouting movement. They come unglued from personal attachments, family connections and romantic relationships. And finally, this 'glue' chips away from abstract things – sanity, health and existence itself. Showing people becoming unglued is a way to show who they really are. Blending in with society, i.e. not becoming unglued, dooms a person to anonymity. WH Auden's 1940 poem 'The Unknown Citizen' is a satirical tribute to a man whose only graces were his utter lack of identifying features. As Auden wrote:

> *Our researchers into Public Opinion are content*
> *That he held the proper opinions for the time of year;*
> *When there was peace, he was for peace:*
> *when there was war, he went*

After illustrating a lifetime of flying beneath the radar, Auden ends the poem with these lines:

Was he free? Was he happy? The question is absurd:
Had anything been wrong, we should certainly
have heard.

Anderson's unglued characters tend not to be
unknown citizens. '[His] dialogue is almost entirely
comprised of things "real" people never say, but
probably think. It's like hearing the gaps between
the pauses in polite conversation', wrote Suzie
MacKenzie. 'I am very sorry for your loss', says Gene
Hackman's huckster patriarch in 2001's *The Royal*

Tenenbaums to his two recently bereaved grandsons. 'Your mother was a terribly attractive woman.'

However these people may suffer, it is rarely in repressed silence. Indeed idiosyncratic characters drive the narratives.

To backtrack, for a moment

Wes Anderson has, to date, written and directed nine feature films. He has made a handful of short features, some advertisements and has acted as producer on three films (his friend Noah Baumbach's *The Squid and the Whale* (2005), his idol Peter Bogadanovich's *She's Funny That Way* (2014) and curiosity documentary project, *Escapes* (2017).

Still, Wes (which is how I shall henceforth be referring to him) is primarily known for his own film work.

A Wes Anderson Feature Presentation x 9 (and some shorts)

The year was 1996 and the movie was called *Bottle Rocket*, which is where our story begins. It was adapted from a Sundance-screened short made with the actors Owen Wilson, Luke Wilson and Robert Musgrave (whatever happened to him?). Wes roped in cinematographer Robert Yeoman, who he admired for his work on Gus Van Sant's *Drugstore Cowboy*, by writing him a charming letter (aside: Robert is not sure how Wes got his home address). It was the beginning of a long-term alliance. Good and helpful people were now on his side. LM Kit Carson (director of the seminal doc-fiction hybrid film, *David Holzman's Diary*, from 1967) joined as producer. The Indian character actor and vaudevillian Kumar Pallana was enlisted for a small role. Andrew Wilson, brother of Luke and Owen, signed up to play jock bully Future Man. The result was a story of friendship, petty crime and first love delivered in Wes's signature deadpan tone, but not his signature look – it is the least symmetrical and stylised of all his works. It offers a showcase for the Wilsons, screen debuts for all three. The film didn't do major business at the box office, which was chalked up to a marketing snafu, but that didn't stop Wes, who rolled out another movie within two years.

Enter Jason Schwartzman, in his first screen role, looking different to how the now-iconic character of go-getting private schoolboy Max

Fisher was initially envisaged (A Mick Jagger type).
Rushmore (1998) is the story of a precocious kid who
pursues too many things and eventually learns to be
satisfied with less. Enter Bill Murray, an established
movie star with a run of largely-comedic big-hitting
roles under his belt (*Caddyshack*, *Stripes*, *Tootsie*,
Groundhog Day, to name but a few). He accepted
to work for a pittance and, indeed, donated $35k
of his own money to achieve a vital helicopter shot.
Seymour Cassel, a character actor known for his
collaborations with American indie godhead John
Cassavetes, joined as Max's father, playing a rare
example within Anderson's oeuvre of a tranquil
male homebody. Enter what would be a recurring

motif of the unattainable love interest/peak of a love triangle in teacher Miss Cross, played by Olivia Williams. Enter elaborate framing devices and a montage introduction (to all of Max's extra-curricular clubs). Enter a uniform that is among those synonymous with Wes's visual iconography – the blazer, tie and glasses.

Next, the scale of production was upped and Wes's birth-state of Texas left behind for the New York of *The Royal Tenenbaums* (2002). This was the director's first bash at working with an expansive ensemble cast which included Anjelica Huston, who would become his joint-most-recurring female player (alongside Tilda Swinton). It also featured a number of single-serving stars including: Gwyneth Paltrow, Danny Glover, Ben Stiller and Gene Hackman. The latter was a disgruntled collaborator who on set yelled accusingly at Wes, 'You promised me I'd be happy!' The film is a character-driven story about a dysfunctional family and the many failures of love. It remains his most overt homage to literary hero JD Salinger, and his first time wading in thematically dark waters – someone dies and there is a suicide attempt. The film is author crazy and book crazy. It is the first of three films which use a book as a framing device for the story.

From New York he sailed off to Cinecittà Studios
in Rome to make *The Life Aquatic with Steve Zissou*
(2004), the first instance of what would become a
personal trend of choosing locations that enabled
him to travel abroad. Inspired by the classic marine-
life documentaries by French oceanographer
Jacques-Yves Cousteau, this was Wes's most overtly
autobiographical work in that the character of
Zissou (played by Bill Murray), as well as being an
explorer, is also a filmmaker and the head of a ragtag
crew. Underlying the adventure story is another
dysfunctional family narrative, as Steve struggles to
be a father to his long-lost son, Ned (Owen Wilson),
and Team Zissou must band together to track down
the Jaguar Shark who killed their beloved colleague
Esteban. Loyal collaborator Murray excels in his
most centrally-billed role, and the character has
since become a poster child for depression. Enter
soon-to-be regulars Jeff Goldblum, Willem Dafoe
and Waris Ahluwalia. The red beanies, silvery blue
wetsuits, custom Adidas trainers, and *The Belafonte*
(a boat whose interior was built from scratch) make
this the trademark aesthetic which even casual Wes
fans recognise. In some ways it is an albatross.

By this point Wes's signature style was sufficiently
established to be ripe for parody. *American Express:*

My Life, My Card from 2006 was, unlike most TV adverts, inspired by François Truffaut's 1973 send-up of moviemaking, *Day For Night*, even using the same Georges Delerue soundtrack. Dressed in a tan suit, Wes himself is introduced with a caption as 'WES ANDERSON, DIRECTOR' in trademark yellow futura font, yelling 'cut, cut, not enough smoke and the snow was too loud', before striding across a movie set, giving precise eccentric orders in a businesslike tone. It works as a funny example of the director retooling his style for a mass-market product while retaining a sense of individual credibility, and it is the first example of many forays into the world of luxuriant commercial-making.

From the heights of absurdity to earthbound railway tracks for 2007's *The Darjeeling Limited* (2007), Wes's most earnest depiction of death and grief. Centred on three brothers, who meet a year after their father's death to travel around India, ostensibly to visit their awol mother, but more urgently to renew their ties. Filmed on location in India, Wes's signature, heightened style was criticised by some as insultingly removed from native reality. The film was set aboard a moving train and was created by 'method-writing' – Wes, Jason Schwartzman and Roman Coppola wrote the

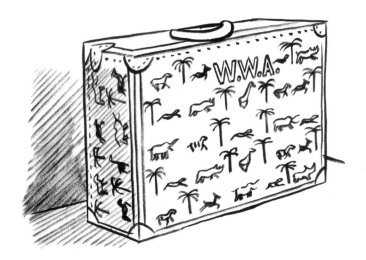

film while travelling around the locations visited by their fictional counterparts. *Hotel Chevalier* arrived alongside the main feature as an optional Chapter 1, and sees Schwartzman's character liaising with a young woman (Natalie Portman) in a hotel in Paris. This doleful short features splotches of rich yellow and is set to Peter Sarstedt's 1969 ballad, 'Where Do You Go To My Lovely', which is played on repeat.

After melding sincerely with more adult themes, Wes in 2009 then burrowed underground into a foxhole of childlike imagination, adapting Roald Dahl's 1973 novel *Fantastic Mr Fox* into his first stop-motion puppet feature film. Production was based in the UK, in outdoor locations and at the animation studio 3 Mills in Bow, East London. Wes went on visual-inspiration-gathering reconnaissance missions to Dahl's former residence, Gipsy House, in Buckinghamshire. This is where he began to dot his family cast with A-Listers (George Clooney and Meryl Streep, playing Mr and Mrs Fox respectively), and it also signalled his increasing power within the film industry. The story is Wes's most simple: a family animal battles, existentially, with his wild nature and, literally, with his trigger-happy neighbourhood farmers Boggis, Bunce and Bean. Much admiring praise was heaped upon his mania for picturesque detail as applied within an entirely handbuilt world.

He returned to the USA for *Moonrise Kingdom* (2012) to turn Rhode Island into a '60s time capsule – not that any of his movies are bound by modern rigours, but this was his first overt period piece. It is the tale of two 12-year-olds who fall in love and run away together. He's Sam (Jared Gilman), an orphaned cub scout who wears chunky glasses. She's Suzy (Kara Hayward), a troubled child with a love of pop music and kittens. Sad adults pepper the backdrop, such as Suzy's parents (Bill Murray and Frances McDormand) and a melancholic police captain (Bruce Willis). The film was inspired by Waris Hussein's 1971 film, *Melody,* about two primary school kids who escape from their school in Lambeth, London, in order to marry.

Alongside this came a trio of little ones: *Cousin Ben Troop Screening with Jason Schwartzman* (2012) is a two-minute, meta *Moonrise* promo created for the humour website, *Funny or Die.* Schwartzman's small but tasty character, the authoritative and highly bribable scout-master Ben, takes centre stage to preside over a scout screening of *Moonrise Kingdom.* The humour derives from his ball-busting approach to marshalling his young and uncowed charges. Then came the apex of Wes's obsession with female romantics who, by virtue of their innocent feminine charms, create love triangles as men fall at their feet. The Prada advert *Candy* (2013) is perhaps his silliest work and is notable for marking his first collaboration with the French actress Lea Seydoux who would fill out a small role as a maid in *The Grand Budapest Hotel.* Then another Prada short, this time with more narrative: *Castello Cavalcanti* (2013) is named after a fictional, mid-century racing driver played by Schwartzman, and the story sees him crashing in a town revealed to have been home to his ancestors. Over spaghetti and deadpan conversation, a poignant connection is established. It's a film of bright colours and pregnant pauses.

Capers! *The Grand Budapest Hotel* (2015) is the story of a concierge and his lobby boy who becomes mixed up with the murderous relatives of the concierge's deceased elderly lover. There are chase sequences, a prison break, a grand slalom, and a comedic Ralph Fiennes. The film's aesthetic was inspired by the paintings of romantic landscape artist Caspar David Friedrich (1773–1840) and snowglobe Hollywood backlot portrayals of Europe. The story is inspired by the writings of the Austrian novelist Stefan Zweig, especially 1939's *Beware of Pity*. The film opened the 2015 Berlin Film Festival and went on to become a sleeper hit. There were cameos for all Wes's favourite actors, and for all its confectionary appearances, it takes on worldly matters (which was novel for Wes) within the key interwar timeline.

Come Together: A Fashion Picture in Motion (2016) is a christmas advert for the high-street retailer H&M in which Wes plunders his very own *The Darjeeling Limited*, casting one of its stars, Adrian Brody, as the train conductor forced to create festive cheer at short notice in order to save Christmas Day.

Which brings us, finally, to *Isle of Dogs* (2018), his second foray into stop-motion animation and his second feature to take an interest in more worldly matters. Political corruption, refugees, scapegoats, environmental disaster, disease and famine all push at the edges of this story about dogs exiled to a trash island in a near future Japan. The film became one of his most critically lauded, yet more accusations of cultural appropriation clouded its reception. It was his first film made as the father of a young daughter.

– End of backtrack–

Everything tends toward disorder, except Wes Anderson

Now we are familiar with the work, it's time to dive a little deeper and address a short note about your humble author. The second law of thermodynamics, also known as the law of disorder, states that 'everything tends towards disorder'. This law was not devised with me in mind, but it perfectly encapsulates my worldview. When I was 21 years old, I painted a faceless mermaid swimming downwards, with little bubbles rising up through the blue water that surrounded her. At the bottom of the page, I wrote: 'From the beginning it was never anything but chaos, it was a fluid which enveloped me, which I breathed in through the gills.' This was taken from Henry Miller's *Tropic of Capricorn*. Like Anaïs Nin, (his lover) Miller was a maestro of flowing, sensuous prose, with characters swimming through the thick fug of circumstances which engulfed their lives.

Since, I have gravitated towards artworks which acknowledge that much of life is beyond our control, whether it's a poem mourning how the sands of time are running out ('how few yet how they seep, through my fingers to the deep, while I weep, while I weep' wrote Edgar Allen Poe in 'A Dream Within A Dream') or the existential films of Terrence Malick, in which a protagonist is always searching for an elusive meaning. Sensuality is another means of escape. 'Body am I entirely and nothing more; and the soul is only the name for something in the body', Friedrich Nietzsche famously wrote in *Thus Spake Zarathustra*. Accordingly, I love more abstract works like Lucile Hadžihalilović's 2015 film *Evolution,* Sarah Polley's *Take This Waltz* from 2011, Hélène Cattet and Bruno Forzani's sensual mood piece *The Strange Colour Of Your Body's Tears*

(2013) and anything by the French filmmaker Claire Denis for the rich moods which stir in me sensations that transcend anything that could be ascribed to narrative or storytelling.

So, I'm writing a book about Wes Anderson. His orderly cinematic worlds confound the mess and incoherence of life. How does he do it? His sense of pristine order flies against nature, and also against me.

In studying the methods, thoughts and – above all – the films of this auteur I have alternated between inspiration and despair. Inspiration came from a desire to channel his organisation, concentration and uncompromising delivery of a personal vision. He is admirable in being a lifelong student of other artists. To read a single interview with him is to become acquainted with hordes of muses, living and dead. Harmonising with past masters is a way to acknowledge who came before you as well as a way to avoid spiritual loneliness while embarking on a longform project.

Although writings on the second law of thermodynamics focuses on entropy – the name given to the movement from order to chaos – it flags that the application of 'an intelligent mind' can create order. This order only lasts for as long as the intelligent mind is applied, but while it lasts, harmonious works can be built. This is what Wes Anderson does. He wills magic parallel universes into being, using all he has to create stories free from all but his artistic values. Although the distance between his visions and my experience of life is dispiritingly far removed, and this sometimes makes me feel inadequate (like I could make beautiful things, if only my mind was stronger), at other times the overtness of his efforts steady my resolve and inspire me to try equally hard.

Sharing sadness with an artist

A strange – in some ways true, in some ways false – sense of intimacy is born from studying an artist. I don't know Wes Anderson personally. I don't know his favourite foods or what puts him in moods or possess any of the private understandings that make up a real relationship. I do know that, at some point in his life, his understanding of sadness connected to my understanding of sadness, and that he took the Herculean step of siphoning this understanding into a film strong enough to hold me whenever I have need of it.

I have, since adolescence, suffered some hard-to-pin melancholia. When I feel it, I try to be alone so I can marinate in a sensation I have no will to express in company. I do not run from this feeling. I lean into it. In the words of the Texan animator Don Hertzfeldt: 'I am proud of my sadness because it means I am alive.'

Worse than sadness is alienation, which is a dislocation from your feelings. The best pursuit in this state is to find a work of art that holds personal meaning with the capacity to return your feelings to you, like a hot bath restoring sensation to a frozen body.

The Royal Tenenbaums is one such work of art. I have a particular memory of it bringing me back to life. I was living in Clapton with my then-boyfriend who was at work. It was a Saturday and I had no plans, so the day stretched ahead full of emptiness. I was locked out of human experience when I put on the DVD. Immediately it woke me up. I got tingles sliding into its unrestrained melancholy. I cried and I cried. It felt amazing.

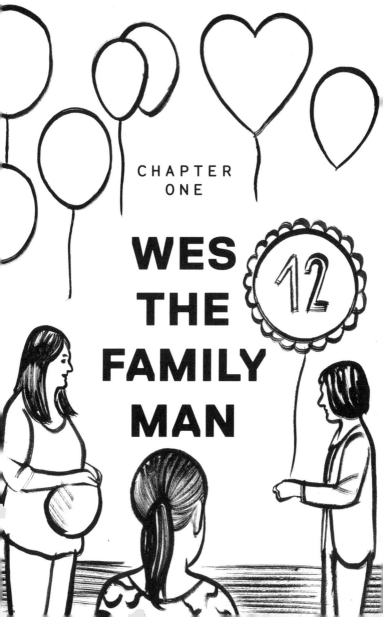

CHAPTER
ONE

WES THE FAMILY MAN

12

IN THIS CHAPTER ...
- Returning to childhood fascinations
  and adventures
- Turning loved ones into collaborators
  and collaborators into loved ones
- Owen Wilson and the gang
- Techniques that make ensemble casts sing

From childhood's hour

When Wes Anderson was 8 years old his dad, who worked in advertising, and his mum, an archaeologist, told their three boys (Wes, Mel and Eric) that they were getting a divorce. This formative event helped to power his third feature, *The Royal Tenenbaums* – the bulk of which unfolds 22 years after Royal and Etheline separate, showing how unresolved familial tension has paralysed their adult children. Chas, Margot and Richie are locked into childhood torments unable to advance their once precocious talents until relations improve and time is casually unpaused decades after it ground to a halt.

Childhood is a state that Wes Anderson has never left behind. He seems particularly nostalgic about the age of 12. It's the age of the little pilot Atari in *Isle of Dogs*, and the runaways, Sam and Suzy, in *Moonrise Kingdom*. This is an exchange from *The Life Aquatic with Steve Zissou*:

> **Jane:** *[about her unborn baby] In 12 years he'll be 11 and a half.*
> **Steve:** *That was my favourite age.*

Wes can remember what it was like to be at that age and overwhelmed by a romantic crush, or when a book could become your whole world. His films always have roles for kids (he is tireless in scouting newcomers, watching hundreds of thousands of self-recorded script readings) and he never condescends to young actors on set. In 2012, Jason Schwartzman – who played a kid in *Rushmore* – said, 'I think he relates to kids.'

Autobiographical details from Anderson's early life are spritzed across his films. This is sometimes the transference of a specific event squirreled away in his computerlike memory and sometimes an adaptation of a cultural sensation that impressed him at a young age. He was a fan of Roald Dahl's

Fantastic Mr Fox decades before he brought the story to the screen. Steve Zissou, from *The Life Aquatic*, is a hybrid of Bill Murray (who plays him) and the explorer-filmmaker Jacques Cousteau, of whom both Anderson and his co-writer Noah Baumbach were huge fans as kids. Their enthusiast perspectives are loaded onto Steve's long-lost-son, Ned, who enters the picture with a naïve respect for a once-renowned filmmaker even though his star is on the wane. As Zissou admits: "I know I haven't been at my best this past decade." But like Ned, Wes doesn't judge a hero character for being weaker than his once bulletproof image would suggest.

A thirst for adventure is part of what drives him. Wes likes to demonstrate action sequences, physically performing the movement about to be filmed in order to guide watching actors or animators. "I think his moviemaking comes from a desire to experience all these things and to live in them," said Schwartzman. Mark Waring, an animator on *Fantastic Mr Fox*, described how Wes acted out every character in the feature script. Footage included on the Blu-ray features him wearing what appears to be a dressing gown, showing how Mr Fox should bite the neck of a doomed chicken. He slowly grabs the imaginary beast, speeding up as he mimes the act of repeatedly biting into a neck. On top of acting, he is narrating stage directions and describing the camera movements as he envisions them. It's beguiling to witness a man operating in a normal environment while reacting to fantasy cues, especially when a large bank of screens spring up, each one containing images of Wes acting out a different character. 'Sometimes you had five Weses in shot, performing five characters,' said Waring. 'You could probably get a film of Wes acting everything out.'

Someone's actively living

For all that he is driven to realise scenes from his imagination, Wes is grounded in reality. He knows what conditions need to be in place for his cast and crew to cooperate in the delivery of a stylised film.

As with one of his heroes, Robert Altman, Wes fosters a deep sense of community. During shoots everyone typically lives together, eats together, talks together and plays together. Actors have heralded the quality of evening meals on his productions ('When you work with Wes you eat well,' said Ralph Fiennes). This communal vibe is a cherry for actors used to the self-sufficient grind of driving to and from Hollywood film sets every day. 'I like the creativity that goes into the life that goes into the making of the film,' said Bill Murray in 2015 when asked why he keeps collaborating with Anderson (he has appeared in 7 of the director's 9 films). 'It's nice

to come along to that kind of a gig where someone's actively living.'

His film sets are full of artists feeding off one another's talents, functioning as a helix for art and life. It's like a hall-of-mirrors where real concerns are reflected as characters' concerns and redeemed, at least in the moment of creation, by the recognition of what art can offer. It's not just Wes draining the lifeforce from his collaborators. In *The Life Aquatic with Steve Zissou*, Intern 1 (of 'don't point the gun at him, he's an unpaid intern' fame) was, indeed, Wes Anderson's unpaid intern, and for his troubles was permitted to make a behind-the-scenes short film. Matthew Grey Gubler's *Life Aquatic Intern Journal* shows that Owen Wilson brought in a foosball table for the cast to rattle around between their scenes. More revealingly, we see how Anderson is a quietly focussed figure on set. In one behind-the-scenes vignette Jeff Goldblum, Willem Dafoe, Michael Gambon, Anjelica Huston, Pawel Wdowczak, Waris Ahluwalia, Bud Cort, Seu Jorge, Cate Blanchett and Noah Taylor are all squashed inside a tiny submarine, their chatter, after a light explodes, dominates the footage while Wes amiably lurks in the back of the vessel. What comes across from Wes's presence in these scenes – as well as in the longer Albert Maysles-directed making of doc, *This Is an Adventure* – is how fixated he is by performance, and also how interested he is in anchoring character dynamics to personal meaning. On the director's commentary for *The Life Aquatic*, he says: 'Generally a lot of personal experience goes into these characters because these movies aren't adapted from something else, they're just made up and they come from our lives.'

The head of a film family

Famously, Anderson uses the same collaborators over and over. Robert Yeoman, his cinematographer, has shot all of his live-action movies. Mark Mothersbaugh (formerly of the surreal rock band Devo) scored everything until the composer Alexandre Desplat grabbed the baton at *Moonrise Kingdom*. Jeremy Dawson, now a producer, has been on board since *The Life Aquatic*. Pawel Wdowczak has been sound mixer on six pictures, and in fact plays a sound mixer in *The Life Aquatic*.

Just as Wes takes professionals and incorporates them into his life, so too does he take people from his life and incorporate them into his pictures. This trait was most visible in the early days before he developed international clout. He cast his then girlfriend, Jennifer Wachtell, to play the fleeting role of Chas's dead wife in *The Royal Tenenbaums*. He scouted the poet, performer and juggler Kumar Pallana from a coffee shop he frequented with the Wilson brothers, and turned him into a recurring cast member. (Kumar's son Dipak also appears in *Bottle Rocket* as a doctor and in *Rushmore* as a teacher).

Family members are enlisted. Real experiences are incorporated. Owen Wilson shot his lesser-

known brother, Andrew, with a BB gun when they were kids resulting in a pellet becoming permanently lodged between his knuckles. This mishap was transferred wholesale to Chas in *The Royal Tenenbaums*. Andrew acted as Chas's hand double, and also donned a beard to play Margot's biological father whose sole scene involves accidentally chopping off her finger. Eric Anderson, Wes's younger brother, is an artist whose services are used for prop and décor design. Among other things, Eric created all the fantasy book covers in *Moonrise Kingdom* and painted the following mural that covers the walls in Richie Tenenbaum's bedroom: set against a sky blue backdrop, images float in cloudbursts of pastel detail. Above a mantelpiece heaving with trophies is a large painting of Royal, Richie and a trophy inside a lawn-green circle. Dotted around the other walls are smaller images that vary from tiger, to envelope, to ice-skate. All are annotated in writing too small to decipher.

How does Wes wrangle his extended family to direct his private visions into being? He is exacting. There is no off-script improvising. Costumes are not to be messed with. Marks are hit. Wes will listen to suggestions but he usually politely declines. On the set of *The Life Aquatic*, Jeff Goldblum – thrilled by finally having a suggestion accepted – mimed Wes picking up a grape with a precisely curved thumb and forefinger saying, 'just this one champagne grape'. Willem Dafoe had one piece of feedback land for *The Grand Budapest Hotel* in which he plays the murderous, leather-clad villain, Jopling. Anderson had written Jopling to have vampire teeth coming down from his upper jaw. Dafoe thought this was clichéd and suggested that he have pointed lower teeth – and this was accepted!

Still, unlike famous tyrants of cinema, the Alfred Hitchcocks and Stanley Kubricks who terrorised their actresses in pursuit of perfect takes, current evidence suggests that Wes manages to realise his visions without terrorising his collaborators – a real plus. 'On some level a director has to be a good general', said Willem Dafoe in 2015, 'and he's a beautiful general. The troops love him and he's clear about what he has to do.'

Owen Wilson and the gang

The term Wes uses to denote collaborators he has worked with repeatedly is his 'gang'. His voice is nonchalant, amiable and halting as he says this word, aware that he – with his delicate bones and lanky elegance – doesn't scan as a typical gang leader. Bill Murray is in the thick of things, along with Jason Schwartzman, Seymour Cassell, Anjelica Huston, but he was not in on the ground floor. To trace Wes's film family back to its roots is to stare into the convivial green eyes of Owen Wilson. The pair met while studying at the University of Texas. Speaking in Paris in 2017, Wes said: 'If we didn't meet – if we didn't click in that way – we would've tried to do one thing or another, but it would've been a harder struggle.' The pair co-wrote *Bottle Rocket*, *Rushmore* and – to an extent – *The Royal Tenenbaums* before Wilson gravitated towards a career as a mainstream comic actor. His last meaty role in an Anderson flick was as the older brother of three, Francis, in *The Darjeeling Limited*, although there have been bit parts in *Fantastic Mr Fox* and *The Grand Budapest Hotel*.

There was once a time when Owen Wilson served as the director's on screen avatar. 'Look how excited he is', is the line that ushers in his very first screen role in Wes Anderson's very first feature, *Bottle Rocket*. As Dignan, he is crouching in the bushes outside a psychiatric hospital holding binoculars and a mirror, poised and ready to help his friend Anthony (Luke Wilson) escape. Anthony is being formally discharged and is free to leave, but indulges his friend by dutifully tying together sheets in order to abseil down one storey to the ground. His doctor comes in to say goodbye and asks about the sheet rope. Anthony points out Dignan in the bushes in an attempt to persuade the doctor to let him leave through the window. 'Do it quickly,' says the doctor. 'This doesn't look good.'

The parallels between Owen and Wes extend further. Both were the middle child of three brothers, both had fathers in advertising and both attended

private schools. On screen: Owen's characters are often the itinerary-wielding driving forces behind schemes – just as Wes occupies this role on the other side of the lens.

Wilson's qualities are embedded in the DNA of the Wesiverse. This is most overt in films that he co-wrote yet, according to a director's Criterion Collection commentary of *The Royal Tenenbaums*, the Wilson Sensitivity is something that guides the director. He has attempted to recreate their close and conversational working style with other writing partners, namely Noah Baumbach (*The Life Aquatic with Steve Zissou, Fantastic Mr Fox*), Jason

Schwartzman (*The Darjeeling Limited*, *Isle of Dogs*), Roman Coppola (*The Darjeeling Limited*, *Moonrise Kingdom*, *Isle of Dogs*) and Hugo Guinness (*The Grand Budapest Hotel*).

A place for everyone

In a Q&A in Paris in 2017, an audience member asked Wes a ballsy question: 'Are you happy with the films you've made?'

'Who ... who said that?!' Wes said, drawing a laugh as he searched the audience with a hand above his eyes, curious to identify the rogue inquisitor.

Having located them he proceeded: 'That's a hard one. I don't know, I don't know. I can say I am happy with all the collaborations that I've had. I'm happy with what other people have done for these movies and I've loved the process of writing these movies with my collaborators.'

Love of collaboration is evident by the way Wes values ensemble bonds. Even movies not directly about families, or even humans, are buoyed by communal values, such as proud loner-stray Chief coming in from the cold to serve the lost 'little pilot' Atari in *Isle of Dogs*. Each character is given space, no matter if they are single-serving or centre-stage. Everyone gets comic lines, everyone gets dramatic gravity, everyone gets style, everyone gets the burden of sorrow.

Technical decisions are also designed to be inclusive. Anderson shoots widescreen, meaning he can place lots of characters in the frame at the same time. He also likes to use montages as a method of itemising the number of souls in his stories. There is no sequence that demonstrates his montage technique more powerfully than Richie's attempted suicide in *The Royal Tenenbaums*.

What precedes the attempt is a scene in a private detective's office. Margot's husband, Raleigh (Bill Murray), rightly suspecting infidelity, has hired a man to snoop on his wife. Richie, secretly in love with Margot, muscles his way into the investigation. Also present is Raleigh's young investigative subject, Dudley. The detective presents an account of Margot's romantic history. She has had many ex-lovers. Her current one is Eli Cash, Richie's best friend.

Richie walks out of this office. The first aching strums of 'Needle in the Hay' – Elliott Smith's heartbroken elegy to his struggle with heroin – begin

to play underneath the next scene. 'Taking the cure, so I can be quiet whenever I want' – these lyrics possess an escapist logic that is transferable to a suicidal urge.

There are two phases of montage: the first takes place in Raleigh's bathroom. 'Needle in the Hay' plays full blast as Richie trims his hair, applies foam and shaves. 'I'm going to kill myself tomorrow', he whispers, removing the blade from the razor. A montage – edited to match the tempo of Smith's strums – provides a stream of images which are his deepest memories, connecting Richie to his mum, his dad, his pet falcon, Mordecai and, of course, Margot. He slices his wrists in an act designed to separate him from them forever.

Then comes the second phase: he is found, slumped and bloodied, by Dudley. The music abruptly stops as Dudley lets out a silent scream (this being a comic relief's moment of emotional gravity). It restarts in a hospital as unconscious Richie is rushed towards camera on a gurney pushed by medics and Raleigh, who wears a blood-streaked hospital gown. Dudley bounces at the rear. Then, in perfect time to Smith's now forceful strumming, we spend a few seconds with each Tenenbaum as they receive the news and rush to be with Richie.

There is so much emotion in each performance: Murray's face sags and his eyes are coloured with grief; Anjelica Huston bolts like a frantic animal from the telephone; Ben Stiller, previously a caricature of clenched anger, allows his eyes to glisten with unshed tears which lend his face a childlike openness; Gwyneth Paltrow raises her voice for the first time. When all of these people are edited together, it provides an overwhelming sense of distress. It shows that familial love can be primal just as it shows that familial love can't stop a man from wanting to die. It isolates each individual character, evoking their essence in a heightened way. It binds them together.

CHAPTER
TWO

WES
THE
ARTIST

Defining the signature

To the casual observer, Wes Anderson is the director who makes symmetrical images. This quality cannot be denied. It is so true that the first thing regular cinematographer, Robert Yeoman, does on set is figure out precisely where to place his camera in order to ensure a centralised image.

'It's not something that I feel is important dramatically, it's just for me,' said Wes, speaking in 2017 in Paris, 'The way I might arrange things in a frame, I compare it to handwriting. You might try to write very well but really you have something that your brain is inclined to do.'

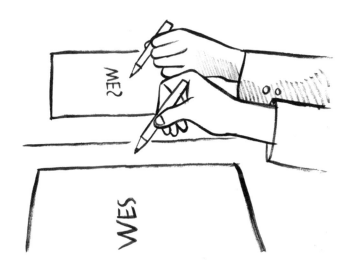

Wes's brain is inclined to keep characters front and centre. Drama doesn't develop subtly in a corner. When it's time for information to be imparted about a character, they will be afforded the full support of a frame. Tableaux or montage convey parcels of emotional information in the fewest possible images. 'His films look like stage plays', wrote the filmmaker and writer, Kartina Richardson, in her 2012 article for *The New Inquiry*, 'Wes Anderson's Arrested Development'. '[The] sets look like sets, the frame becomes the proscenium arch (a symmetry in the set that exaggerates and enhances the frame's boundaries), and the action is kept in the centre of the frame, usually directed out toward the audience in mainly medium or wide shots.'

He may not deem it a place for human drama but Anderson does not ignore the background of his frame. He is so obsessed with detail and the integrity of a single prop, that everything you can see has a backstory. Royal Tenenbaum lies to his adult kids by saying that 'he has a pretty bad case of cancer' in a scene where the camera begins by focusing on a painting of a red-headed nurse posed against a blue background. She has a determined stare which goes directly into the lens, her back is straight and her hands are clasped. She is supposed to be Royal's mother, but this is never made explicit within the film. After a few beats, the camera pans down to show Royal sitting at the head of a table looking out at Margot, Richie and Chas. The rest of the scene, one of conflict between Royal and Chas, is shot from a lower vantage so we do not see the painting again. Still, it was specially commissioned and a model posed for it, because nothing in existence would serve the purpose. And so it goes – the decor of every room is considered. Originality is key. Adding visual texture or a storytelling layer is vital. All of Wes's movies require repeated viewings because the extent of the worldbuilding is too exhaustive to appreciate in a single sitting.

Style is the ultimate emotional camouflage

In the course of researching and writing this book, I have many times been awestruck by the scale of Wes Anderson's artistry. The pre-planning that goes into the pre-planning which goes into the planning which goes into movie-making is such that it's hard to imagine him wasting time or succumbing to any mental affliction (stress, egotism) which can derail the focus of a less organised mind (this writer would know). How did he come to be this way? What does he get out of stylising sets, costumes, camera movements and dialogue in ways that sometimes complement his themes and sometimes distract from them? Why does he spend months developing a prop that will appear in the background of a scene for a few seconds?

We will likely never know the answers to these questions. Wes is more interested in building worlds than in laying bare his own one – which isn't to say that he lacks emotional depths, rather that he camouflages

those depths within a bigger picture, never dialing back his theatrical style to expose something naked and quivering. He is open in acknowledging that his stories are inspired by life experiences, but he is also a hardcore cinephile who looks to bygone masters – like a technician would refer to a manual – when considering how to transform ideas into images. So, while all his characters are serious and sincere, the manner in which their dalliances are stitched together is gleefully constructed. He amplifies individual malaise with evocative costumes and casts actors who can convey rich swathes of feeling in a look or a delivery. If there is one word for his artistic values it is: elaborate.

Any sense of who Wes is amid all this machinery is a glimpse of a shadow caught in the corner of a funhouse mirror. And yet he is there – unmistakably – in every frame.

Turning recognisable locations into personal worlds

Bottle Rocket and – to some extent – *Rushmore* are slight artistic outliers in that they take place in settings recognisably of this world. Thereafter, locations take on a fantastical hue. *The Royal Tenenbaums* is set in New York but pains were taken not to use any famous landmarks. Gene Hackman was baffled when they shot a scene by the Hudson River with Kumar Pallana strategically placed to block out the Statue of Liberty. Likewise there were concoctions and inventions – all characters travel by Gypsy Cab, there is a 305 St Y (which doesn't exist) and existing locations were repackaged – The Lindbergh Hotel, where Royal lives and later finds gainful employment as an elevator operator, uses the lobby of The Waldorf Hotel. The young Richie and Margot run away to spend the night in a museum which in reality was a set-dressed bank foyer.

Wes's approach to world-building grew in his first foray into stop-motion puppetry, *Fantastic Mr Fox*. Despite extensive preparations being integral to the Anderson operation, when it comes down to live-action shooting, he works with a small crew in the form of a single department. For *Fantastic Mr Fox* there were 29 departments. Research began with a thorough inventory of the late Roald Dahl's former home, Gipsy House , where all his books, proofs and widow, Felicity Dahl, still reside at time of writing. Wes drank up all this real-life stimuli by taking photographs of every object in the house. He would later go through the images, selecting what was aesthetically suitable to be modelled in miniature and used in the movie.

'He loves the idea that he can really create every bit of the image that's on the screen,' said Jeremy Dawson, a producer on *The Darjeeling Limited*, *Fantastic Mr Fox*, *Moonrise Kingdom*, *The Grand Budapest Hotel* and *Isle of Dogs*. Dawson has a background in visual effects (he worked on *The Life Aquatic* and across five Darren Aronofsky titles in this capacity). 'Somebody coming from a live action background is used to a set dresser having a bunch of things sitting on the table and you'll be like, "What can we put on this table?" and they'll pull out this vase or this coffee cup. Here we're having to think about this in advance. Wes'll say, "Let's make a coffee cup that looks like this coffee cup I saw in a restaurant in New York".'

The *ne plus ultra* of Wes's world-building is his second stop-motion puppetry creation, *Isle of Dogs*. Set on a trash island, with human rubbish providing tactile surroundings, there are scenes set amid mountains of coloured bottles, each of which was handmade. Lead figures in the graphic design and puppetry departments spent close to three years crafting tiny objects and figures for what turned

out to be an elaborate animated dollhouse filtered through the aesthetic of a garbage dump!

Fussy attention to detail does not correspond to being an oppressive force. 'I loved being at close quarters to the precise way that Wes gathers everything together', said Ralph Fiennes, talking in 2015. 'It's the camera position, it's the set, it's the props.' He then turned to Wes who was beside him. 'But also you bring everything together – all these actors – and it seems to me that you then want

them to bring their own individual imagination, and talent.'

Growing into a look

Once upon a time in a land far, far away, Wes Anderson didn't dress in tailored suits, and didn't have the haircut of an Edwardian brat. He shot *Bottle Rocket* in 1996 wearing jeans, and with glasses and short hair. Likewise, characters wore casual clothes, although his taste for using costume items as comical props is seen when Dignan doles out women's hosiery for everyone to wear on their heads in a small time robbery. As time has passed, uniforms have become integral to his cinematic visions, and have extended to include himself. The most satisfying instance of synchronicity is the fact that Wes owns the exact same brown suit as modelled by Mr Fox.

The cottage industry of impersonating a Wes Anderson character

Fancy dress parties across the world have been visited by women with kohl eyes and fur coats; by his-and-her costumes with him in a cub scout uniform decorated by merit badges and her in a sixties mini-dress, Sunday-school shoes and binoculars; and by lots of people in little red hats. It's possible to buy the white and blue Team Zissou trainers and the luggage found in *The Darjeeling Limited*. Heck, even my friends who don't work in the world of film have drunk from the sartorial well of Wes. My expertise is rarely sought in life, but I was once called upon to advise on the fancy dress options for a female who didn't want to go to a party as Margot Tenenbaum or Suzy Bishop. For what it's worth, I advised adopting Inez from *Bottle Rocket*'s white hotel uniform. (This advice was not taken.)

What is the meaning of this?

Wes strives to make every frame, every character and every object iconic. What is the impact of such carefully choreographed image-making? A symbolic moment takes place midway through *The Grand Budapest Hotel*. M Gustave has been slung in jail where his exquisite manners enable him to befriend his swarthy cellmates. Together they plan a breakout. But how to smuggle in the tools necessary for their escape? M Gustave has an idea involving the artisan choux pastry business, Mendls.

In his review for *The Telegraph* in 2015, Tim Robey opened with this line: 'In his new comedy, *The Grand Budapest Hotel*, Wes Anderson has found an elegant solution to gripes about how stifling, how annoyingly perfect, his films can

be. He ignores them wholeheartedly.' Indeed, with its pastel palette and old-world European architecture, *The Grand Budapest Hotel* is an Andersonian fairy-tale which eats itself. The whole resembles a delicate pastry castle – something that might have been dreamed up meta-style – by Herr Mendl, whose apprentice, Agathe (Saoirse Ronan), sends escape tools to M Gustave by embedding them within choux pastries. So perfect are her creations that a guard who has been taking a cleaver to lesser foodstuffs sent from the outside cannot bring himself to dissect these pristine confections. The pink Mendls box is waved through intact.

Could the creation of perfect images be a self-preservation technique? A way to ensure that, regardless of what's happening inside of his movies, their surfaces are so delightful that knife-wielding critics cannot callously hack them to bits? Barbs can (and are) flung: 'Wes Anderson's nostalgia, like his set design, is so contrived that I don't believe he really believes in anything but visual style', wrote Anwen Crawford for *The Monthly* in 2015. But it's not so easy to entirely dismiss a work so clearly the product of hours, day, weeks, years of meticulously focussed labour.

Making order out of chaos

Dignan is a man who likes to make lists. No sooner has he 'broken' Anthony out of a psychiatric unit, than he is revealing a 75-year plan for how they will approach social survival before and after their crime spree. The list is written in a notebook in orange and blue felt tip pen and is broken down into these subheadings: Initial Five Years, The 2nd Five Years, 3rd Phase Years 10-15, The Next 25 Years, The Next 50.

Lists, maps and assorted handwritten plans are a fixture of Wes Anderson's movies (all penned by his fair hand), as characters earnestly attempt to forge their dreams through the medium of organisation. 'I had Brendan draw us up an itinerary', says a heavily injured Francis to his brothers in *The Darjeeling Limited*, in almost the same breath as telling them that he loves them more than anyone else in the world. His itineraries are laminated and contain a logo for 'francis whitman industries' even though they are intended to only be seen by family members. It is as if formal composition will lend a legitimacy to what is simply one man's will, which sounds a little autobiographical. 'When you're making a movie, you're not just organising the chaos, you're creating a new chaos which is the chaos of trying to make a movie,' said Wes Anderson in Paris in 2017. 'And the one thing that I've enjoyed learning to do, or figuring out little aspects of, anyway, is making some systems for just running a movie.'

CHAPTER
THREE

WES
THE
ROMANTIC

IN THIS CHAPTER ...

— Steering clear of dirty sex

— Putting women on pedestals

— Chanson d'amour

— The romance of impossible love

Coitus interruptus at Hotel Chevalier

I t is understandable that an artist preoccupied with creating order out of a messy world would steer clear of graphic sexual entanglements. The most adult depiction of romance in his body of work is of one its death-throes. The short feature *Hotel Chevalier* – an optional part 1 to *The Darjeeling Limited* – lasts just 11 minutes and stars Natalie Portman opposite Jason Schwartzman who plays his *Darjeeling* character, Jack. (Portman appears in *Darjeeling* in a dream montage of the train's passengers). He is holed up in a hotel in Paris. She – his ex-girlfriend – has tracked him down there. On hearing her knock at the door, he, like many an Andersonian romantic lead, presses play on a song he's cued up to set the tone. In this instance it's 'Where Do You Go To My Lovely' a 60s ballad by Peter Sarstedt. He opens the door to the first lyric: 'You talk like Marlene Dietrich ...'. She's standing there on the phone. 'I'll talk to you later,' she says to whoever's on the other end, before laughing, 'What is this song?' They hug very closely. The camera catches a pang on her face.

These are characters in a limbo state between breaking up and moving on. The atmosphere is loaded with chemistry and barbed by unspeakable hurt. From her guilt and his brittleness, it seems like she was the one who broke up with him. Yet she is here now, prowling around his quarters, brushing her teeth, taking in his room as he takes in her presence.

'If we fuck I'm going to feel like shit tomorrow', she says.
'That's okay with me', he says.

This exchange comes while she is on top of him in bed. It also comes after he – sitting on the bed as she stands before him – peels off her pants and strokes her naked butt, a large green-purple bruise on her pale flesh drawing attention to itself in the frame. We soon see another bruise on her arm. The inference is that she's had rough sex with someone else.

Despite his callous talk, Jack gives her an easy out from their intimate physical situation, asking if she wants to see his view of Paris. We cut to a slow-mo sequence. She is naked but artfully posed as Sarstedt starts up again. He approaches and tenderly wraps her in a yellow hotel robe. They make their way to the balcony. They look out at the city: together, perhaps for the last time.

It is telling that a scenario with all the narrative momentum of a sex scene and which, in another auteur's hands would have ended in post-coital bleakness, swerves away from fluids and climax and la petite mort and towards a moment of chaste togetherness.

A pedestal overflowing with romantic female types

Wes Anderson romanticises women, even when they are stop-motion dogs or foxes. He does it in a way that is idolatrous but that strips away the chaotic forces that guide his men. Women are rarely the reckless adventurers or brooding antiheroes at the centre of a narrative. His most-used female player is the incomparable Anjelica Huston. She has appeared in *The Royal Tenenbaums*, *The Life Aquatic* and *The Darjeeling Limited*, acting as a statuesque source of female strength amid a sea of befuddled men. Such are her skills for making characters come alive that she can transform a low-key role into something iconic. As Etheline Tenenbaum, she is the force that has kept the family together by reliably showing up for day-to-day duties ('You're true blue, Ethel.') and generally being the opposite of roguish son-of-a-gun Royal.

In *The Life Aquatic* she is a more dramatic character. Eleanor Zissou is an heiress with a streak of blue in her hair – this detail was decided upon by costume designer and former Stanley Kubrick

collaborator, Milena Canonero. Yet once again, her major narrative function is to save the day: funding the mission with her family nest egg after Ned's fortune is stolen by pirates. Only in *The Darjeeling Limited* is she a more flawed character, as a woman who flees her family not once, but twice. Even so she is barely on screen, and the film leans heavily on her ability to be staunch and compelling.

As both Etheline and Eleanor, Huston stirs jealousy by having two men interested in her at once. This is a recurring scenario for female characters, especially the younger, angel-faced ones, who seem to be catalysts for men acting out their melancholy and wounded pride. Women are prizes to be fought over (Miss Cross in *Rushmore*, Margot in *The Royal Tenenbaums*, Jane Winslett-Richardson in *The Life Aquatic*) as they look on with sad-eyed helplessness, trying not to indulge the petty hysterias of the men, but afforded little other function within the narrative.

Out of the mouths of babes

Only the kids are alright. Suzy in *Moonrise Kingdom*, and to a lesser extent Agatha in *The Grand Budapest*

Hotel, are caught up in the same capers as their little men. As such, their liaisons play out on equal footings. Suzy and Sam's love story was inspired by Wes remembering the feelings he had for a girl at the age of 12. As with most events in his life, he has a vivid recall of the scenario's specifics and of how it was all-consuming ('A 12-year-old with a crush, that's really the whole world for that person.').

The heartfelt script gives the orphaned cub scout, Sam, and binoculars-wielding bookworm, Suzy, the redemptive love that they deserve. Indeed, Wes shows affiliation for his young female character by ascribing to her an event from his own childhood: she finds on top of a refrigerator in her family home a pamphlet called, 'Coping With The Very Troubled Child' which is clearly about her. It's a prop that has since become a staple at Anderson-themed fancy dress parties and spawned a line of luggage (used in *The Darjeeling Limited*) but here it is fully weaponised as a source of pain and disconnection. It shows up twice: the first time in a confessional moment when she shows it to Sam and he makes the mistake of laughing, and the second once she's been taken back home and her mum is bathing her. On seeing the pamphlet peeping out of Suzy's bag, Frances McDormand, with a voice full of sorrow says, 'Poor Suzy, why is everything so hard for you?' Suzy responds with the defiant non-sequitur, 'We're in love and we want to be together. What's so wrong with that?'

What's telling is that these 12-year-old bonds are purer and more conducive to happiness than the ones we see in the adult world. Suzy's mother is having an affair with, 'that dumb, sad policeman' Captain Sharp (Bruce Willis). When her husband Walt (Bill Murray) finds out, what follows is one of the bleakest scenes in Wes Anderson's oeuvre.

Murray has been playing variations of caustic, flawed, domineering, lost men in every Anderson movie where he's had a significant role. Here, as Suzy's father Mr Bishop, he is physically present in that imposing body, but emotionally he has gone somewhere private. His eyes are ringed with purple circles from an earlier accident which makes him seem haunted. He and Mrs Bishop – who has just wrapped up her romantic affair – lie in separate twin beds and stare at the ceiling. A hurricane is drawing in and dancing tree branches cast shadows on the ceiling. Angelic choral voices sing notes of warning. In the middle of an exchange about work, Mrs Bishop gets real:

> *"I'm sorry, Walt ..."*
> *"It's not your fault ... Which injuries are you apologising for, specifically?"*
> *"Specifically, whichever ones still hurt."*
> *"Half of those were self-inflicted ... I hope the roof flies off and I get sucked into space. They'll be better off without me."*
> *"Stop feeling sorry for yourself."*
> *"Why?"*
> *"Because we're all they have."*
> *"It's not enough."*

This is a relationship in which the couple have grown so distant that the one who has been cheated on cannot pretend that the affair is the root of their problems. This is a man whose awareness of his own inadequacies means he doesn't blame his wife for wanting more. The contrast between this despairing state of separation within a marriage and the hot-blooded, hot-headed union between the 12-year-olds is a clear vote for the way that youth do things. Given that adult unions are stymied by death or divorce in a further four titles (*Rushmore, Tenenbaums, Aquatic* and *Darjeeling*) it seems fair to read a certain amount of wistfulness within the Wesiverse for the simplicity and strength of childhood feelings.

Flooding the frame with songs of love

In *Bottle Rocket*, Anthony, wearing swimming shorts, paces around the edges of the motel pool, and throws his white towel off to the side. His movements are captured in a long shot. He dives into the water. At that moment, it switches to an underwater camera and upbeat Latin music begins – 'Prendeme La Vela' by Abelardo Vasquez and Cumanana. The screen is filled with the colour blue until the blurry shape of Anthony swims towards the lens, and gradually shifts into focus. Cut to a poolside shot that shows Anthony surfacing with wet hair. (Luke Wilson has a sweet little bob in this film). He leans on the side of the pool, distracted in thought. Then something grabs his attention: a woman in a white dress. She hasn't seen him. She is pushing a big industrial sheet trolley. A wobbly zoom into Anthony signals that he is transfixed. As she moves, his eyes follow her. His expression brightens, like he has just been told that he aced an exam. She tosses her hair and smoothes it into a ponytail. She strokes her bare leg with her foot. The Latin music is emanating from her radio. Then she clocks him. He gives an amiable little wave. She thinks, flashes a half smile and then disappears into the next room on her rounds. He deliberately falls backwards into the water in a swoon.

Most romantic moments – at least according to one character's perception – arrive with their own musical signature. One rainy night in *Rushmore*, Max Fisher appears at Miss Cross's bedroom window. He has applied fake blood to his head and claims to have been hit by a car in order to con her into admitting him to her most private of chambers. She disappears to collect medical supplies. He gets comfortable on her bed before removing a tape from his blazer pocket and popping it into her tape-deck. 'Rue St Vincent' by Yves Montand fills the room. On her return, he forces a kiss before she realises

the blood is fake and furiously throws him out. The scene is disturbing because of his deception and comical because of Max's delusions. The music represents an ideal he aspires to rather than a feeling they share.

This is not the case across all the romantic moments. When the yearning throbs of 'Le Temps D'Amour' by Françoise Hardy play, Suzy and Sam dance in their underwear and taste sex for the first time in their private Moonrise Kingdom. The minor-key melancholics of 'These Days' by Nico soundtracks the moment when Richie and Margot Tenenbaum clap eyes on one another after years apart. In both cases, the flush of the music captures something true about these relationships.

The skulduggery of straight men

Supportive, functioning relationships are few and far between. An exception is the spouse of Mr Fox. Mrs Fox is a steady hand at the tiller – but she is both a character that Wes inherited from Roald Dahl and a woman. And female characters, as we have covered, are often simplified and placed on a pedestal. Other stable relationships are presented not as subjects in themselves, but to emphasise more volatile scenarios. Henry Sherman (Danny Glover, sporting a dignified salt and pepper baby fro) has been Etheline's accountant for years, and what's more, wrote the excellently-named book, *Accounting For Everything*. He is all that Royal isn't and, indeed, the pair have many a scuffle as the former tries to weasel his way back into Etheline's good graces.

There are a fair number of inadequate male would-be lovers, whose manipulative attempts to win the objects of their affection lead to scrapes with love rivals. Or, in the case of Max Fisher, a scrape with the object of affection herself as Miss Cross manages to secure him in a headlock after he tries to kiss her in a classroom. Men are presented as morally lacking when it comes to endearing themselves to women: Royal lies about having cancer; Max lies about having been in a car crash; Steve Zissou lies about the rules of life aboard *The Belafonte*. Their female love interests are presented as good-hearted but suspicious, and the men are usually exposed and sent away. Uncomfortably, there are no queer relationships, but Wes is comfortable putting homophobic slurs in the mouth of his male antiheroes, so we have: 'bulldyke', 'fruit', 'closet queer', 'Gay little earring' floating awkwardly on the surface of otherwise heteronormative worlds.

The romance of impossible love

Wes likes to present would-be lovers in a doomed scenario that enables him to explore the tooth-gnashing anguish of desire. His preference for the chaste unions that spring up between adolescents becomes a taste for impossible desire when characters grow up. There are no thriving, hot-blooded, adult relationships in his entire output. His movies are saturated with longing, but he is less interested in the sweaty physical fulfillment of this longing than in the picturesque pining that is flung up by the presence of an elusive muse.

The most edgy relationship is the one between adoptive brother and sister Margot and Richie Tenenbaum, who were originally planned to be flesh-and-blood siblings. The final set-up is less taboo, 'but still frowned upon', (as Royal says). 'I think that the characters I most relate to are Margot and Richie,' Wes said on a director's commentary for *The Royal Tenenbaums*. 'She's going through something that's almost an adolescent feeling. Richie has something soulful.'

'I think we're just gonna have to be secretly in love with each other and leave it at that', says Margot, peering through the door of the tent she has just left at Richie who lies there still propped up on his elbows. He has come from the hospital after surviving a suicide attempt. She was the cause ('but it's not your fault'). They have finally confessed their feelings after decades of silence, talking, kissing and lying frozen together as two Rolling Stones records play: 'She Smiled Sweetly' and 'Ruby Tuesday'. This resolve to end a relationship before it has begun, or, rather, to feel love without consummating it is pure Andersonian romance. He finds poignance in connections that are drifting away, or preserves an emotional sensation by not draining it dry. As Ted Hughes wrote in his poem, 'Fidelity':

I think of it
As a kind of time that cannot pass,
That I never used, so still possess.

The intimacy that turns Wes on is the type you can possess. It is a sensation that enables you to float above this world unchallenged by earthly mess. Yes, characters hook up, but more often than not they also have to say goodbye, and the images of their time together are asset-stripped for nostalgic intensity. Rather than comfortable togetherness, he favours yearning solitude. Love is not for everyday life, it is the most loaded picture in a photo album dedicated to a moment long since passed.

'And now I want to die'. [takes a bite of a biscuit]

CHAPTER
FOUR

WES
THE
SUCCESS

IN THIS CHAPTER ...

— The early crash of *Bottle Rocket*

— Discreetly becoming a magnetic force

— A feeling for failed characters

— The personal nature of artistic success

The rise, fall and rise of Wesley Wales Anderson

was never more confident in my life than when we made that film and never less confident than when we screened it', said Wes Anderson talking about his 1996 feature debut *Bottle Rocket* to his pal and two-time co-writer, Noah Baumbach, in 2010. When *Bottle Rocket* was first completed, he was a young man high on imagination. He'd been creative since childhood, conceiving adventure and spy stories with his two brothers, and assembling amateur footage into collages. Hell, he even cut a hole in the roof of his family home for one shoot. The sky was literally the limit.

Then came university and the discovery of a simpatico creative soul in Owen Wilson, who he met in a playwriting class (his core course of study was in philosophy). He directed his new friend in enough trial scenes to be impressed by Wilson's acting. After graduating from The University of Texas the pair teamed up with Owen's brother Luke and spent years hustling the short version of *Bottle Rocket* into being. Producing help came from mentors that included James L Brooks (whose laurels include being a three-time Oscar winner and writer on *The Simpsons*) and LM Kit Carson (a writer, actor and producer whose credits include *Paris, Texas*, *The Texas Chainsaw Massacre 2* and *David Holzman's Diary*).

His short, *Bottle Rocket*, screened at Sundance, and off the back of that, $5 million was raised to expand it into a feature. Wes was feeling very good about his stature as a filmmaker while attending a test screening of his first full feature in Santa Monica. As he told Baumbach:

'We screened it at the AMC for an audience of 400 people. As the reels unspooled – I was sitting in the back row with all the studio people – I began to see people leaving. They were leaving in groups. People don't go to the bathroom in groups. They're not coming back. They take their coats ... And it

became really excruciating. At a certain point, I left. I tried to be very discreet about it because I didn't want to add to the exodus feeling, but I also couldn't take it. I went up to the projection booth and watched. They left all through the film and it was really a miserable thing.'

Though loose by the standards that now define Wes Anderson, *Bottle Rocket* was a strong calling card, powered by tragicomic characters and a spirit of adventure. Martin Scorsese gave it retroactive kudos in 2000 when, on the show *Roger Ebert at the Movies*, he named it as one of his favourite films of the '90s. At the time of release critics appreciated it. Kenneth Turan of the *LA Times* raved that it was: 'A confident, eccentric debut ...

that feels particularly refreshing because it never compromises on its delicate deadpan sensibility.' Still, it bombed at the box office, and it was not until Anderson's second feature, *Rushmore* (screen debut of actor Jason Schwartzman) that it became clear he had a significant future in the business.

Eight features later and over 20 years on, his reputation has steadily evolved to the point that he is one of a handful of auteurs free to command productions without studio interference. He harnesses his gleaming rep mainly by drawing household name actors over to his sets, sometimes for mere minutes of screen time. He is respected on the arthouse circuit (*Moonrise Kingdom* was the opening film at the Cannes Film Festival in 2012) and known by casual cinemagoers, whose support made *The Grand Budapest Hotel* a sleeper hit in 2015. He has achieved the dubious distinction of being worthy of satire. The reddit thread *Accidental Anderson* of aesthetically pleasing sites from around the world, was born in April 2017. He has been spoofed on YouTube where individual users have remade trailers of movies, such as *Harry Potter* and *X-Men*, in his geometric, deadpan style. His own friend, Edward Norton, helped *Saturday Night Live* to develop a spoof horror film called

A Midnight Coterie of Sinister Intruders. He is so embedded within film culture that his name has a public meaning that is independent of his work.

THE MIDNIGHT COTERIE OF SINISTER INTRUDERS

Within the biz, he is a private person in the sense that there are no pap snaps of him stumbling drunk off Leonardo DiCaprio's yacht, or otherwise entertaining the social opportunities available to the rich and famous. Yet he possesses a powerful network. His habit of befriending those he works with and working with those he has befriended means that his film family has become a dynasty. He is in with the Coppolas. (Roman Coppola and Jason Schwartzman are regular collaborators and he counts Sofia as a friend.) He is able to court A-Listers (George Clooney, Meryl Streep, Bruce Willis) and indie darlings (Tilda Swinton, Willem Dafoe, Edward Norton). Having achieved success on his own artistic terms, he is at the peak of his powers and unfazed by the trappings of fame, using it only to draw in collaborators. *Isle of Dogs* boasts glittering Wes newcomers: Scarlett Johansson, Bryan Cranston and Greta Gerwig. Still, bigger names are thrust into idiosyncratic roles just the same as more anonymous co-stars. 'There isn't any time along the way when it really mattered to me whether or not the last movie I did was better-known than the one before or anything like that,' said Wes, 'It's really just doing the same thing I've been doing for years, just on a new story.'

Where do you go to, my lovely?

'As a director it isn't like you've been on any kind of career track', said the beloved *New York Times* journalist, David Carr, in an on-stage interview with Anderson and Ralph Fiennes, conducted shortly before Carr died: 'The only thing you've ever set out to make – it seems to me – is a Wes Anderson film. As a director or actor it's usually, "one for them, one for me." You never do the one for them.'

'You're right', responded Wes. 'Well, part of that is this: It's not like I'm fending off all these offers. They go to Sam Mendes, they didn't go to me.'

'I'd like to see your Bond movie.'

'I have one. Do you wanna hear it? I had this one I wanted to do called Mission Deferred. My idea is that the Cold War is over and there's no gig. He goes in to see M and M is on the phone and he's walking around M's office. The gadgetry is ... he has a great coffee machine, and maybe he gets into a bar fight or something because he has a license to kill. And so, um, I never got the call.'

This speech works equally well as a serious movie pitch and a pastiche of Andersonian sensibilities. Anderson is a consummate deadpan and fully capable of satirising himself, however for my money he is serious and, given the chance, would make a Bond movie in which nothing happens.

Falling head-over-heels to the lowest level of failure

Steve Zissou, clad in a silvery-blue Team Zissou polyester wetsuit, misses a step and tumbles forward, rolling down the stairs of Hotel Citroën. The building is decrepit, with foliage and animals populating what were once glorious rooms. In better days, Steve came here with his first wife, Jacqueline, whom he loved so much that he tattooed her name onto his body and christened a submarine after her. But she didn't really love him. Birds fly as Steve lands with a resounding thump at the bottom of the stairs. He stays where he has fallen, lying prone, arms spread-eagled.

'Did you get that, Vikram?' he asks a man with a movie camera. With Steve is a small crew, also wearing silvery-blue Team Zissou wetsuits, and all peering down from the top of the stairs.

'Uh yeah', says Vikram, training the camera on his fallen boss.

'Good,' says Steve. 'We'll give them the reality this time: a washed-up old man with no friends, no distribution deal, wife on the rocks, people laughing at him, feeling sorry for himself.'

From this humiliation onwards, there is a slight softening of Zissou's arrogant manner. Failure runs through Wes's work, especially his first four films. Only his most two-dimensional character, the cocky but charming Mr Fox, gets to be upwardly mobile and succeed without being forced to deepen his appreciation of his place in the world.

Dignan fails at his criminal endeavours and ends up in jail, where he finds a sort of contentment. Max Fisher gets kicked out of his beloved Rushmore and focuses on his theatrical career instead. The Tenenbaums kids peaked too soon, lived for decades in disillusionment, then rediscovered a will to live while older and wiser. Similarly, Steve Zissou had outlived his star power, although he still tries to trade on it. All the dogs on trash island are socially ostracised – cast aside from their destiny of being man's best friend.

Failure, and in particular acknowledgement of failure, lends characters grace notes absent when they don blinkers and gallop towards the perceived rewards of success. Failure awards the perspective that happiness exists in places where callow youths who are desperate for recognition cannot anticipate. Disillusionment is not all bad – to shed illusions is to become wise. To fail in one area does not mean that

all is lost. As Arthur Golden writes in *Memoirs of a Geisha*:

'Adversity is like a strong wind. I don't mean just that it holds us back from places we might otherwise go. It also tears away from us all but the things that cannot be torn, so that afterward we see ourselves as we really are, and not merely as we might like to be.'

The fleeting nature of all of life's achievements

The Grand Budapest Hotel is full of melancholic awareness that, as the *Rushmore* motto goes, *sic transit gloria*: glory fades. An establishment that was once the embodiment of visual splendour, social capital, and one man's destiny is – as the film begins – a husk of its former self. In the Communist present of the film's timeline it is a cavern with draughts that blow nostalgia through its uninhabited corridors. It falls to Zero, a survivor of these olden days to, first: shed a tear over his saddle of lamb and, second, to tell the story of when The Grand Budapest Hotel was the jewel in the crown of Zubrowska. He assures that no one was more instrumental in realising this state of affairs than the honourable concierge

M Gustave. Wes built this film after discovering a location he scouted in Görlitz, Germany, on the Polish border. In the wistful ambience that colours the narrative bookends is a present which reminds us that all this too shall pass. And it shall be this way, even for those who, like Wes, are currently living their dreams. Films preserve stories and collaborations, but the people who make them are as much at the mercy of time as anyone. As the British film director Terence Davies once said: 'At the peak of ecstasy, we are in decay.' This sensitivity is present in Zero's narration. It seems like Wes Anderson isn't enmeshed in ecstasy.

What does success mean to our man?

'The central event of my life is getting to make movies.'
– Wes Anderson, 2005

To an aesthete like Anderson, making movies is synonymous with corralling the mess of life into beautiful, orderly, tragicomic cinematic frames that hang together as a story and enable him to collaborate with friends. Wes doesn't like to work alone. Owen Wilson's star took off when he was supposed to be co-writing *The Royal Tenenbaums*. As a consequence, Wes wrote most of it alone in a hotel room. He 'hated' working that way. Considering the egotism rampant among directors, it is refreshing to hear of the emphasis Anderson puts on collaborating: 'Shoots are a way to get to have reunions.'

Our ideals of success surface in youth when we have no control over our lives and therefore the freedom to fantasise over what we will do once in charge. For most people, adulthood involves compromising these fantasies. With Wes it is possible to trace childhood dreams to adulthood reality. For example, when he was 12 years old and living in Houston, Texas, he presented his divorced parents with handouts detailing why it was high-time for him to move to Paris. Mentally, he was ready to make the move, but his parents felt it was too soon. Fast-forward to the present moment and Wes Anderson is living in Paris with his Lebanese-English artist girlfriend, Juman Malouf. They have a daughter named after a character from Frank Borzage's *The Mortal Storm*. It would be a perfect happily-ever-after, if only 'The End' existed like it does in the movies.

CHAPTER FIVE

WES
THE
STUDENT

IN THIS CHAPTER ...

— Learning movie-making by watching movies

— The many inspirations for *The Royal Tenenbaums*

— Head teachers Louis Malle and Francois Truffaut

— The film library on *The Grand Budapest Hotel*

The world is just about enough

'**W**ith each movie I have a different set of inspirations', said Wes Anderson in 2012.

Wes didn't go to film school. His film education is built into his lifestyle which involves engaging with filmmakers, artists, writers, photographers and assorted creatives, both alive and dead. Wes's films are an evocation of what is burning up in his other interests as a cinephile, scholar and world traveller. He does not embody that cliché of a starving artist locked in a garret giving birth to solitary fever dreams. He is a worldly gourmand, who spices up his imagination by cherry picking from those far-flung buffets which are available to the culturally-keen globetrotter.

The dynasties behind
The Royal Tenenbaums

There are a cornucopia of inspirations which preempt each and every Wes movie. Considering how they spark off each other is illustrative of his process. '*The Royal Tenenbaums* was really inspired by *The Magnificent Ambersons* more than anything,' he told Matt Zoller-Seitz. *Ambersons*, made by Orson Welles in 1942 (the year after *Citizen Kane*, the film which eventually propelled its maker into the annals of cinema history), is a sprawling, tragic tale of an initially prosperous Indianapolis family whose wealth and happiness take a swan dive together. Based on a 1918 novel by Booth Tarkington, Welles gave the film a bleaker ending, which was reshot and recut while he was working on another project in Brazil.

A similar title construction between *The Magnificent Ambersons* and *The Royal Tenenbaums*

is immediately apparent. They both share gravelly voiced narrators – Orson Welles himself in the former, his 1990s equivalent, Alec Baldwin, in the latter. Also the set-up of the house, the faded glory, the dysfunctional ancestry which all but destroys itself. Wes ran with the idea of eccentric dynasties and familiarised himself with two gems from the 1930s. The first is *The Royal Family of Broadway* (1930), directed by George Cukor, which is a thinly veiled but loving satire of the Barrymore acting family and based on a play by Edna Ferber and George Kaufman. *You Can't Take It With You* (1938), directed by Frank Capra, sees

James Stewart and Jean Arthur playing would-be lovebirds from families with clashing values (his snobbish, hers idiosyncratic). Boasting the tagline 'You'll love them all for giving you the swellest time you've ever had!' it scooped the Best Picture and Best Director gongs at the 1938 Academy Awards.

The concept of grand families permeates his casting choices: Gwyneth Paltrow is the daughter of Blythe Danner, a Tony-Award winning Broadway actress. Anjelica Huston is so thoroughly marinated in show-business that she is the third generation of the same family to win an Academy Award (her director father, John, and actor grandfather, Walter, came before). Wes is interested in people, inasmuch as he is interested in characters. He feeds off their qualities in order to invent fictional roles. Wes told Zoller-Seitz that the part of Richie was written for Luke Wilson because of his unusual combination of popularity and privacy: 'He's a very charismatic person, and he certainly doesn't wear his heart on his sleeve.'

He told a story to illustrate what fascinates him: 'When Luke got sent to boarding school, he was saying that no one there liked him. When Mr Wilson got there, what he saw was that Luke was one of the most popular kids in the school – but

Luke just didn't feel that appreciation I guess. He was sad, and he was homesick, and he didn't want to be there.' This quality of being cocooned in an emotional state far away from loved ones is amplified in the character of Richie, whose distance is such that, when the film begins, he has left his family to live on a boat at sea.

The Royal Tenenbaums is also a soul twin to JD Salinger's short stories about the Glass family published in the 1950s and 1960s. The married surname of one of the Glass children, BooBoo, is Tannenbaum. The idea of child prodigies who achieve social celebrity then spend decades in mournful obscurity is pure Salinger. On top of narrative similarities, there is a shared atmosphere

of delicate melancholy fuelled by characters who know that their intelligence won't save them from the spiritual emptiness of contemporary American life.

There are also cosmetic nods to other works. Richie's line, 'I'm going to kill myself tomorrow', is lifted from Louis Malle's sensationally despairing 1963 film *Le Feu Follet* (based on a 1931 Pierre Drieu La Rochelle book). On a lighter note, Wes entertained himself by taking the line, 'I know you, asshole', from Peter Weir's 1985 film, *Witness* – a link is that both films star Danny Glover.

These little hat-tips to past masters are blended into the narrative of Wes's movies meaning the film – like a sturdy barn (cf *Witness*) – doesn't topple if you can't keep up. He happily reveals the sources of stray lines or compositions or camera angles as a way to keep his forebears in the spotlight. He is equally candid when it comes to influences that helped to create each of his films. I am delighted to include at the end of this book, an Amazon-like 'if you liked x movie you may also like y movie/book/ painting' so that curious readers can engage with the cultural works that helped to inspire Wes's cultural works. At this exact moment, however, I would like to pay lip service to three men whose influences run so deep that they don't exist as a surface reference to be picked up, and instead are mixed up in the soul of everything that Wes has created.

Some passages on the two head teachers at Wes's film academy

On the occasion of *Rushmore* receiving a special edition DVD release in NYC, the studio wanted to screen it at a party in its maker's honours. Wes refused, saying everyone had seen *Rushmore*, and suggested they screen *Murmur of the Heart* by Louis Malle instead. 'It's a movie that I feel very

comfortable being associated with because I feel so connected to it', he said.

This is a big thing to say about a movie that frames incest as semi-natural. Set in Dijon in the 1950s, *Murmur of the Heart* follows the growing pains of Laurent, the youngest in a family made up of two lawless older brothers, a distracted father and a young, beautiful mother. The film rides an atmosphere that is warm and spiky. Laurent's brothers have an anarchy that could erupt into danger at any moment. His mother is loving but too carefree to be trusted. Malle conjures the void that exists between even the closest people. When Laurent eventually loses his virginity to his mother it is treated as an aberration but an understandable one given their need for intimate contact.

Malle was active in the 1950s to the 1990s and made a huge range of films. His 1958 feature debut, *Elevator to the Gallows*, which gave Jeanne Moreau her screen break, is a sleek crime thriller with a Miles Davis soundtrack and is indistinguishable from the zany larks of *Zazie dans le Métro* which arrived two years later. He made films about love (*Les Amants*), suicide (*Le Feu Follet*), war (*Au Revoir Les Enfants*), dinner (*My Dinner With Andre*) and a series of documentaries about India. He worked with explorer Jacques Cousteau on an aquatic documentary, *The Silent World*, which won the Cannes Palme d'Or in 1956 and an Academy Award in 1957.

Despite, or perhaps because, of his shapeshifting approach to filmmaking, Malle never achieved the same recognition as his French New Wave peers and is a more opaque historical figure than, say, François Truffaut or Jean-Luc Godard. For Wes, with his palatable and recognisable signature, to pledge allegiance to this stylistically elusive director is surprising until you consider the emotions that turn both on.

Both are compelled by childhood, especially sensitive children who navigate the wilds of growing up with their eyes wide open. Their heady innocence

eventually turns into adult weariness. The elegant spiritual heaviness of Alain in *Le Feu Follet* aligns with the grown-ups in Wes's worlds. A continuum beginning with youthful hope and ending in adult heartbreak is present in every single film by Wesley Wales Anderson, but shaken into different shapes.

The 400 Blows (*Les Quatre Cents Coups*) from 1959 scarcely needs an introduction. François Truffaut's debut is credited with launching the French New Wave (which is inaccurate as Agnès Varda launched it with *La Pointe Courte* in 1955) and routinely graces Best Films Of All Time lists. In the 1980s, 15-year-old Wes was investigating culture in Houston, Texas, and found *The 400 Blows* in the video rental section of a record store. It was a lightning bolt: 'This movie in particular was one of the reasons why I thought that I would like to make movies,' he said speaking at The New York Public Library in 2014. 'This is such a personal story and it's the director's story. It's like a first novel. It's his, and it is also very emotional, very alive.'

Truffaut had done a whole lot of living before he transferred some of that life to the shoulders of Antoine Doinel, his alter-ego played by Jean-Pierre Léaud in a total of five films: *The 400 Blows, Antoine and Colette, Stolen Kisses, Bed and Board* and *Love on the Run* (known collectively as *The Adventures of Antoine Doinel*). Raised until the age of eight by his grandmother, Truffaut subsequently struggled to adjust to life with his mother and stepfather (his biological father was unknown) and spent a lot of time away from home discovering cinema. He was expelled from school at 14, dabbled in petty criminality, served in the army, was arrested for desertion, was bailed out by the film critic André Bazin, became a critic himself, and founded auteur theory with Bazin, all before beginning his filmmaking career at the age of 27.

When an artist lives a dramatic life of public record it's glaring when biographical details pop up in their work. When an artist lives a more refined and private life, like Wes, the biographical details are more subtly encoded. Wes doesn't lay claim to major events in his movies but he accepts that they are informed by the people he knows, the places he's been, the experiences he's had. The nature of his attachment to Truffaut – the fact that an emotional life is what excited teenage Wes about the medium – reveals something about his central point of contact with the work.

Both men are united by self-taught cinephilia and bibliophilia. Decades before Wes raided the

University of Texas library to learn about European arthouse directors, Truffaut was hitting Henri Langlois' Cinémathèque Français, and discovering American directors like John Ford, Howard Hawks and Nicholas Ray. Meanwhile François was an antecedent to Wes as a user of books as set dressing. *The Royal Tenenbaum*'s title card of one book cover repeated is lifted from the 1971 film *Two English Girls*.

When the student becomes the teacher

On the set of *The Grand Budapest Hotel*, Wes had a film library open to those involved. 'He never formally screened them [the movies]', reported Willem Dafoe. 'He just said they are available. There was only one copy of each so it was like, if Ed Norton is hanging on to *To Be Or Not To Be* too long, I'm going to break into his room and get it.'

To gain an insight into what it's like to browse through Wes's inspirations, this intrepid writer took it upon herself to watch all the films that we know were in the library in order to see how they were evoked in *The Grand Budapest Hotel*.

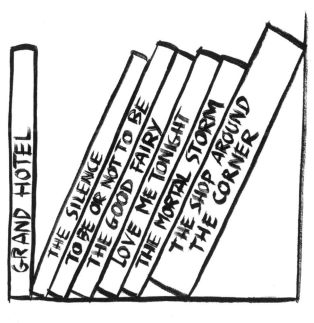

1. GRAND HOTEL

Edmund Goulding (1932)

Edmund Goulding was born in 1891 in the UK but, like so many who were drawn to the bright lights of Hollywood, died in LA. *Grand Hotel* was his hit and one of the biggest box office smashers of the early '30s. A glittering cast includes Greta Garbo, Joan Crawford and not one but two Barrymores (Lionel and John) which makes it a melodramatic illustration of old Hollywood razzmatazz. For want of a better word, it's a hoot. Lionel Barrymore's character, a dying man determined to live out his final days well, adds existentialism ('Life is wonderful, but it's very dangerous …'). The setting of a hotel in Europe (Berlin to be precise) provides an overt parallel with *The Grand Budapest Hotel*.

2. THE SHOP AROUND THE CORNER
Ernst Lubitsch (1942)

Ernst Lubitsch was a genius whose skill for visual comedy and elegant storytelling has never been equalled. In 1922 he moved from Berlin to Hollywood where he made silent films and then talkies until his death in 1947. His talents were duly exalted in his day, but his legacy has since been eclipsed by filmmakers such as Billy Wilder, who followed in his giant footsteps. *The Shop Around The Corner* is Lubitsch's best known film, serving as an alternative Jimmy Stewart Christmas film to *It's A Wonderful Life*, and updated in 1998 by Nora Ephron as *You've Got Mail*. The small group of employees at the Matusheck & Company department store are a service industry family with a deep compassion underlying their professional manners, which is the dynamic that colours employees at The Grand Budapest hotel. Both films use wit as the trojan horse to smuggle in a great sense of malaise. Screwball comedy sets the tone, but darkness and loneliness skulk beneath these poised characters and their hectic worlds.

3. TO BE OR NOT TO BE

Ernst Lubitsch (1942)

'I've left the fate of my country in the hands of a ham', says a director to his leading man. It is Warsaw, 1939 and a theatre troupe is trying to intercept a Nazi spy by impersonating Nazis themsleves. Lubitsch's brilliant satire drew complaints of tastelessness on release in 1940 and it's hard to imagine any film more equipped to receive the criticism of 'Too soon, bro'. Wes is less breathtaking in the taboos he tackles, though he still draws on confrontational irreverence by mixing M Gustave's refined speech with vulgar outbursts and references to sex with elderly women. Both films share a giddy delight in comic delivery, blocking, rhythm and a seamless switching of focus between the low-stakes but important-to-the-characters matter of their public facing professions and the violent dangers present in the worlds they navigate.

4. THE GOOD FAIRY

William Wyler (1935)

William Wyler is the biggest commercial success story in the Wes film library in a record-holding type of a way. At time of writing no one else but Wyler has won the Best Picture Academy Award three times — he did it for *Mrs. Miniver* (1942), *The Best Years of Our Lives* (1946) and *Ben-Hur* (1959). *The Good Fairy* arrived early in his career and is a below-the-radar credit on his lengthy and celebrated filmography. With a screenplay by wisecracker-in-chief, Preston Sturges, and a starring role for Margaret Sullavan (who Wyler married during filming), it poses as a romcom, but the conceit — a naive orphan navigating desirous men — plays uneasily today. There are echoes of its fast-paced, capertastic tone in *The Grand Budapest Hotel* and, like Sullavan's Luisa, Zero is an orphan trying to survive by being helpful and dodging bullets.

5. LOVE ME TONIGHT

Rouben Mamoulian (1932)

Rouben Mamoulian was born to an Armenian family
in Georgia in 1897 and died in LA in 1987 having
made his most lauded artistic contributions
in the first half of the 20th century in the
form of plays, movies and, most especially,
musicals. His reputation suffered a blow after
the US critic and author Andrew Sarris filed
him in the Less Than Meets The Eye chapter of
the 1968 book *The American Cinema*. Still, as
one of the early sound directors, Mamoulian's
name has secured its place in history. *Love Me
Tonight*, his fourth movie, is a musical which
stars Lubitsch regular Maurice Chevalier as a
Parisian tailor who falls for a princess while
posing as a baron. It's possible to see shades
of M Gustave in the tailor whose good manners
and immaculate appearance enable him to move
between different rungs of society with ease.

6. THE MORTAL STORM

Frank Borzage (1940)

Frank Borzage was a prolific director of romantic melodramas, though he acted during the early years of his career. *The Mortal Storm* is one of his masterpieces. Set in Germany in 1933 it succeeds in plotting a moving personal course into a 20th century horror. The sentimental romance between leads Margaret Sullavan and Jimmy Stewart finds a devastating counterweight in the familial tragedy wrought by the rise of Hitler. As critic/director Kent Jones put it, 'in Nazism Borzage finally recognised a formidable enemy of love'. I see a lot of *The Grand Budapest Hotel* in the Hollywood backlot version of Europe – the faux snowy vistas and men with American accents named Fritz and Otto. None of the snowglobe MGM trappings erode the extraordinary human drama and sense of sorrow.

7. THE SILENCE

Ingmar Bergman (1963)

People who don't care about cinema still know
the name Ingmar Bergman. The Swedish auteur is
a towering figure, yet the inclusion of this
particular title within the film library is
baffling. The setting – a hotel in a fictional
European town as war rumbles closer – is
familiar enough. Yet the characters, the tone
and the timbre is not. Bergman's trademark
predilection for extreme close-ups on the
faces of suffering women is evident from the
off as two sisters and a young boy sit on a
train. After they check into a hotel, there are
psychosexual dilemmas, hints of incest and the
resurgence of old family power struggles. The
sheer slowness and uncompromising heaviness of
the atmosphere is the polar opposite to the
mile-a-minute, intoxicating lightness of *The
Grand Budapest Hotel*.

[Class dismissed]

WES
THE
MATRYOSHKA

Opening the curtains on unreserved fiction

Rushmore (the film) begins with blue velvet curtains opening on ... Rushmore (the school). After a prologue, the movie is divided into months via different coloured curtains with the name of the month projected using a xenon bulb. The action begins in September (burgundy curtains) and ends in January (brown curtains).

Wes recounts how he was discouraged from using this contrivance:

'My agent (who I love) was like, "Yeah – you don't need that. That's just a show-off thing. It doesn't help, and it takes you out of the story and the reality of the movie, and I can tell there's a curtain on a movie set there, because it looks like a real thing".

'And I said, "It's *supposed* to look like a real thing."

'"I know, but I can *tell* there's a curtain where you're shooting it."

'"I know!"

'"Yeah, but there's not *supposed* to be. It's supposed to be people, real people."

'And I said, "Well, I know that, yes, but I do want the curtain there." Often what might take somebody else out of it is what I think is the most beautiful thing.'

In *The Royal Tenenbaums*, a similar device is used to remind viewers that we're watching a fictional story. The film begins with a book being checked out

CHAPTER ONE

of a library, a hand (Wes's!) stamps it and then, boom, Alec Baldwin's narration begins: 'Royal Tenenbaum bought the house on Archer Avenue in the winter of his thirty-fifth year.'

The film proceeds in nine chapters and an epilogue. Each new chapter begins with a shot of the words in the book that was checked out of the library (themselves verbatim recreations of the words in Wes and Owen's screenplay.)

Framings are important to Wes. The idea of placing stories inside stories inside stories. *Isle of Dogs*, his most recent film at time of writing, stands as perhaps his most elaborately framed film yet. It is bookended by a prologue and an epilogue and divided into four parts (The Little Pilot, The Search For Spots, The Rendez Vous, Atari's Lantern) which contain flashbacks with specific timeframes, such as 'three weeks ago'. The dogs and foreign exchange student Tracy speak English. The rest of the characters speak Japanese. Instead of using subtitles to enable English audiences to understand Japanese-speaking characters, written and verbal translations run throughout. Labels in English and Japanese pop up on screen framing and illuminating foreign objects. Wes has fun with this function, whether identifying the technology in his near-future Japan (The Rescue

Drone which releases robot dogs) or using the technology itself to spell out a function (when the robot dog's status is switched to LAPDOG the snarling death-beast performs a TRICK). Using words as a visual frame within the frame is a combination of Wes's love of language with his love of order. The union is heady, gripping and hard to fully grasp on a single viewing.

Precision is moving, like Tracy Chapman managing to hold a perfect note while singing about the saddest thing in 'Fast Car'. That's what's awesome: someone composing a note, holding the note, securing the correct instrumentation, and still managing to deliver the feeling in the midst of all that construction. I don't know why composure is more moving than a breakdown. A breakdown is moving in its own way. It's the spectacle of another's pain, but when that pain is refined enough to become a performance, it's like a gift – someone being strong for you, somebody making something *for you*, someone briefly conquering their demons *for you*. Wes does this. He makes it so that you can, with a good conscience, enjoy – not that pain per se, although there's relief in seeing pain, but he makes you feel like it's okay to enjoy it because he's self-consciously constructed so much style. All this labour creates the opposite feeling to the guilty voyeurism of rubbernecking when you see people fighting in the street. Those sorts of altercations are artless. Wes is artful. It's a human impulse to want to connect and relate with other people on a level of pure emotion, and yet when that emotion erupts in real life, it can be overwhelming. Art provides a frame for so much messy human experience. Wes's art provides frames *within frames,* forensically dissecting messy human experience into its component parts, like a scientist of sorrow. His ability to do this is awesome because it shows a brief mastery of that which tears most of us apart. His rendering of sadness is empathetic enough to prove that he knows how it feels, yet his control in the face of this soft and melting emotion reveals an adult steel. Where creators are adult, viewers are free to be children by casting off the learned scepticisms of maturity and relaxing into the hands of storyteller.

Writers published by Anderson and Associates

Wes is a bibliophile as well as a cinephile, and his films are dotted with fictional authors. So literal stories within the stories. Here are some key names that pop up within his fictional publishing house imprint.

MAX FISHER

KNOWN FOR — Using dynamite in a school play

CRITICS SAY — While lacking in maturity and refinement, young Max Fisher shows a compelling boldness and unwillingness to compromise his visions.

ELI CASH
KNOWN FOR — *Old Custer*
CRITICS SAY — Not a genius.

ETHELINE TENENBAUM
KNOWN FOR — *A Family of Geniuses*
CRITICS SAY — Mrs Tenenbaum chronicles
the nuances of human behaviour and shows
remarkable objectivity when evaluating the merits
of her own family.

MARGOT TENENBAUM
NOTABLE WORKS — *Three Plays, The Levinsons
in the Trees*
CRITICS SAY — Ms Tenenbaum is an old soul
whose despair at human nature sometimes
reaches perceptive heights and sometimes feels
excessively maudlin.

RALEIGH ST CLAIR
NOTABLE WORKS — *The Peculiar
Neurodegenerative Inhabitants of the Kazawa
Atoll, Dudley's World*
CRITICS SAY — The once great Raleigh St Clair is
turning to increasingly obscure lines of enquiry.

HENRY SHERMAN

NOTABLE WORKS — *Accounting For Everything –*
A Guide to Personal Finance

CRITICS SAY — It was a pleasure to spend 176
pages in the capable and informative hands of
Mr Sherman.

STEVE ZISSOU

NOTABLE WORKS — *The Sexual Maturity of*
the Moonfish

CRITICS SAY — These companion reads to
Zissou's documentaries are full of fascinating facts
about the natural world.

JACK WHITMAN

NOTABLE WORKS — 'Invisible Ink' and other
short stories

CRITICS SAY — It's hard to resist the suspicion
that Mr Whitman is working out some emotional
issues on the page.

MR FOX

NOTABLE WORKS — 'Fox about town with
Mr Fox'

CRITICS SAY — Breezy, charismatic, forgettable.

What creative recognition does and does not buy you in life

'Why would they make a point of saying I'm *not* a genius', asks Eli Cash down the phone, following the publication of his latest book, *Old Custer*. He is wearing an outfit made up of cowboy hat, fringed jacket, loud shirt and shoes with no socks. There is a tinge of hurt in Owen Wilson's lackadaisical delivery, as he digests this critique, although he remains capable of scrawling his autograph on books held out by passersby, without making eye contact.

Cash is styled like a modern cowboy in a way that looks ostentatious, even in a Wes Anderson movie. *The Sunday Magazine Section* (the fake magazine which splashes him on their cover) bills him as 'the James Joyce of the west'. He is a rare success among the authors in Wes world, making enough money to burn a portion of it on mescaline, a large collection of pornographic films and some eccentric quad-bike based artwork.

Although his social status exists in contrast with the burn-out Tenenbaum adult kids, the poignance of his character stems from the fact that being a writer was always a means to something else, never a shining goal in itself. What he really wanted was recognition from the clan that lived across the street. "I always wanted to be a Tenenbaum," he admits to Richie in a lovably hangdog fashion. Eli thought writing success would be a passport to the heart of their family, but no Tenenbaum is particularly interested in his literary ascent.

Wes's writers rarely find fulfilment in their occupations. Writing tends to be at best a consolation prize and, at worst, a distraction from more urgent pursuits. What Wes's precocious, creative characters desire is something warmer than the cold comfort of publication – something like contact, love, reassurance, connectedness. The fallacy that once legacy is achieved the rest will follow causes immense suffering (in Eli's case it leads down some unsavoury alleys) and an imbalance between what a person has in reputation and what they have in the most private quarters of their lives.

Wes seems to be wise to what recognition does and does not bring. When Matt Zoller-Seitz asked how he connects to the world that receives the films that he slaves over, his response was impressively ego-light: 'I want people to go see my movies, and I'm very eager to have people like them ... But how much good can come from putting any time into studying how people are responding? The best-case scenario is that it makes you feel flattered for a certain period of time, which doesn't really buy you much, in life. Inevitably, it's not going to just be the best-case scenario, so learn to spare yourself that experience.'

If we believe what he says then he does not waste time trying to slake a thirst for public validation. I'm inclined to believe him because vanity is a timesuck and his labours are so demanding that there can't be much time left over for preening. Or rather preening could be ruinous to his creative goals. All these seemingly harmless ways of idling herald a slow death to creative goals, because time is all we have to make good.

An extravagantly long but necessary digression on the work of JD Salinger

A poster child for the private life of the creative soul

Jerome David Salinger achieved intense fame in the wake of the publication of his first and only novel, *The Catcher in the Rye*, in 1951. This was a personal story that Salinger, drafted to the US infantry during World War Two, worked on throughout his service. He had the first six chapters of the manuscript with him on D-Day according to Shane Salarno, co-author of the 2013 biography, *Salinger*. Salarno believes, 'he carried it with him almost as a talisman to keep him alive'.

The Catcher in the Rye's 16-year-old narrator, Holden Caulfield, is believed to be a vessel for much of his creator's formative experience. He is an impossibly exacting and sad teenager who, as the yarn begins, has been kicked out of yet another school, and delays encountering the disappointment of his parents by burning all his money on an impulse-driven spiral through NYC.

Journalists dogged Salinger for interviews. Producers hounded him for film rights. He evaded their attentions, and removed himself from New York City, relocating to Cornish, New Hampshire where he remained until he died. In the intervening decades he published a tiny corpus of work, which included *Franny and Zooey* (1961), two short stories bound together on the turmoil of the once brilliant Glass children, and several short story collections, three of which also featured the Glass family. *Raise High the Roof Beam, Carpenters* and *Seymour: An Introduction* was the last volume ever to be published with his blessing in 1963.

Salinger knew that publicity didn't buy much. He invested so little in the hullaballoo of recognition that he retired at the peak of his powers. He lived the last 47 years of his life without ever publishing new work. Although he stopped sharing it, Salinger kept writing. In an extremely rare 1974 interview given to *The New York Times* for a piece called 'JD Salinger Speaks About His Silence', he said: 'There is a marvelous peace in not publishing. It's peaceful. Still. Publishing is a terrible invasion of my privacy. I

like to write. I love to write. But I write just for myself and my own pleasure.'

This rhymes with the section of the *Bhagavad Gita* that Salinger quotes in *Franny and Zooey*:

'You have the right to the work, but for the work's sake only. You have no right to the fruits of work. Fruits of work must never be your motive in working.' It's worth noting that the interview Salinger gave to *The New York Times* (his first in 21 years according to legend) was prompted by the appearance, in bookshops, of unauthorised editions of his early short stories. He spoke to the paper to express his displeasure at this turn of events.

Protecting intimate peculiarities by saying no to adaptation

In 1957 Salinger responded to a letter from a Mr Herbert who proposed that Salinger sell him the stage and screen rights to *The Catcher in the Rye*. Salinger says no in such a confiding tone that it feels like a compliment. His letter ends: 'Thank you, though, for your friendly and highly readable letter. My mail from producers has mostly been hell.' Before he gets into that, he provides a description of Holden and why his creation is inherently, unadaptably novelistic:

> *'The weight of the book is in the narrator's voice, the non-stop peculiarities of it, his personal, extremely discriminating attitude to the reader-listener, his asides about gasoline rainbows in street puddles, his philosophy or way of looking at cowhide suitcases and empty toothpaste cartons – in a word, his thoughts. He can't legitimately be separated from his own first-person technique.'*

Salinger was burnt by *My Foolish Heart*. An early short story, 'Uncle Wiggily in Connecticut', featuring the dead Walt Glass, was published in *The*

New Yorker in 1948. The following year its 11 pages
were spun into 98 minutes of silly generic romantic
drama. 'We thought they would make a good
movie', was the scathingly dismissive comment by
Salinger's long-time agent, Dorothy Olding. After
that there were a handful of unauthorised Spanish
language efforts, but no more official movies
adapted from Salinger's books.

Wes couldn't – not even if he wanted to – adapt a Salinger story, but he doesn't need to do anything as direct as transform an existing text when the pair possess such a shared sensitivity. Sensitive, stricken protagonists (some women but mainly young white men with fragile egos) are virtually interchangeable between the worlds of Wes and JD. Both steep troubled characters in understanding and lack of judgment. Characters aren't blamed for struggling with complex disappointments. The sense of the world being a place that will surely break your heart is present across all Wes's films, but his first three are the most strikingly in debt to Salinger. *The Royal Tenenbaums* is related to the Glass family. *Rushmore*'s Max Fisher possesses some of Holden's qualities: his prep school stylings, fencing, the flitting between child and adult worlds and obliviousness to the fact that adults see him as a child.

As Franny does in *Franny and Zooey*, Holden has a nervous breakdown. Maybe it's gauche to slap on that label when Salinger never does. His way of revealing where Holden ends up is so low-key you could easily miss it. In the interior monologue of his hero he writes: 'I could probably tell you what I did after I went home, and how I got sick and all, and what school I'm supposed to go to next fall, after I get out of here ...'

It's marvellously subtle to infer a stint of medically-assisted rejuvenation just by saying, 'after I get out of here'. It works to keep Salinger and his hero's perspectives aligned. Rather than framing everything Holden has said in the book as a symptom of a disturbed mind, his disillusionment stands as an example of what happens when you go into a tailspin at 16 and can't fall into line at school even though you come from a stable home, and your parents are wealthy Park Avenue types.

The opening of *Bottle Rocket* is Anthony leaving a psychiatric hospital, and it could be seen as starting where *The Catcher in the Rye* ends. His pal Dignan has come to 'break him out of there'. After a successful escape, they sit on a bus looking like healthy and wholesome dorks. Dignan has a military-issue flattop and a white buttoned t-shirt, Anthony has long brown hair in a bob and wears a red fleece.

'So, did you enjoy your first visit to the nuthouse?' asks Anthony, in an ironic tone.

Dignan gets very antsy: 'Hey, hey, hey, shhh, shhh, shhh. Be sensitive to the fact that other people are not comfortable talking about emotional disturbances!' He pauses and lest he seem unworldly adds: 'You know I am. I'm fine with that, but, other people ...'

It's a funny outburst, especially in Owen Wilson's chipper drawl, yet it also reveals that the one who just got out of the nuthouse has more chill than the one who didn't, and the former will have to keep his experiences to himself, lest he alarm his friend.

Wes empathises with those who suffer with mental anguish. His protagonists are often melancholic – if not fully depressed. This comes across in the morose dialogue Some actors are directed to be slower in word and deed than their counterparts, not that anyone is *all that* functional in the Wesverse. Perhaps M Gustave, exemplary concierge of The Grand Budapest Hotel, is the most adept at getting things done routinely to a high standard. Still, his origins are a mystery. Our narrator Zero says he never asked where M Gustave came from.

Nothing in this world can stop me worrying about that girl

Like Wes, Salinger had a soft spot for the perspectives of children and their relative purity of heart. Holden finds fault with almost everyone he encounters – people either upset him or strike him as false. One exception is his sister, Phoebe. She's only ten and has red hair. 'You should see her. You never saw a little kid so pretty and smart in your entire life.'

Anthony has a kid sister in *Bottle Rocket*. She's called Grace and has red hair. He visits her at school to ask her to return earrings to their mother (which Dignan stole during a break-in). In what is perhaps a nod to Salinger, Anthony interrupts Grace talking to a friend called Bernice. (Holden finds a note of Phoebe's that reads: *Bernice meet me at recess I have something very very important to tell you.*)

Both girls have more gravitas than their wayward older brothers. Despite their youth they know more about social conformity and are distressed by the spectacle of their brothers diverging from the correct path. Although Grace and Phoebe are helpless to prevent what happens from happening, their presence in the stories provides poignant comic moments. Luke Wilson is about three times the size of actress Shea Fowler, but she reprimands him in a stern voice after he claims that he was in the nuthouse for exhaustion. She pierces his emotional truth with a brutal, social one, asking how he could be exhausted when he never worked a day in his life. Equally, Phoebe gets so mad at Holden after finding out that he's been kicked out of Pencey Prep, she refuses to look at him by hiding her head under the pillow. A small person in a big mood is a touching sight to behold, especially when their mood is inspired by a fretful kind of love. Wes persists in having little and large pairings in most of his movies which, on the one hand, are sight gags, and on the other hand, illustrate that adults have more in common with children then they might like to admit.

The shadowy homes of adult children who peaked too soon

The most glaring crossover between JD and Wes exists through the Glass family and *The Royal Tenenbaums*. There are seven Glass children (Seymour, Buddy, Boo Boo, Walt, Walker, Franny, Zooey), two of whom are dead (Seymour and Walt), and three Tenenbaums (two and a half if you consider that Margot was adopted). Both broods were child prodigies who become public property – the Glass children dominated general-knowledge radio-panel-show *It's a Wise Child*, while the young Tenenbaums were top dogs in high-finance, playwriting and tennis, as chronicled in the book by mother Etheline, *Family of Geniuses*.

These achievements are in the past of characters shown as adults struggling with grief, depression, unrequited love and a host of other complications. The thesis is: you may fly close to the sun, but you can't live up there. Instilling the idea that you can in a young mind makes the eventual fall all the more perilous. In *Franny and Zooey*, Zooey regrets the idealistic education that he and Franny received from older brothers Seymour and Buddy. 'I'm a twenty-five-year-old freak and she's a twenty-year-

old freak, and both those bastards are responsible', he says to his mother, Bessie. The Tenenbaum kids are scarred by their parents divorce, and Royal's subsequent abandonment of them all.

These families, even though they are dysfunctional, hold an eternal pull. The Tenenbaum children flock back to the nest, just as Franny, after collapsing on a bad date, returns to the home where Zooey lives with their parents. The adult children find old rooms frozen in time, with their formative years preserved via electronic tie-racks, posters, or a scroll of inspirational quotes on how to live. There is comfort in a space that acts as a time capsule for who you used to be, even if it also provides a reminder that you haven't evolved too much, and maybe even have lost something you used to have. Returning to a personal nucleus is a kind of retreat, but carries the hope of domestic progress, be it a bridge built with a relative, or reconciliation with the shadow of our former selves.

Progress in *Franny and Zooey* is slight. After going through the ringer Franny finds a reason for a private smile, redolent of the smile of Melora Walters flashes at the end of *Magnolia* (another film by another Anderson, featuring a depressed grown-up version of a former child prodigy in Quiz Kid Donnie Smith of *What Do Kids Know?*) *The*

Royal Tenenbaums depicts a more revolutionary type of progress: estranged family members learn to trust one another and certain emotional tragedies become less disturbing.

The importance of feeling the rich kid blues

If you're doing okay socially and have nothing to worry about materially but still feel bad, it can be hard to justify those blues to yourself. There are plenty of hardasses who would dismiss this type of abstract malaise as trivial in comparison with real-world suffering. The ineffable sense of things being slightly out of whack is of glaring importance to the person under this impression but nearly impossible to communicate to others in a convincingly weighty fashion. Yet this private language of the heart is what keeps the lights on inside, and if you shut yourself down in that way, it is a silent death, like when the roots of a tree are severed but it takes years to fall to the ground.

The reason why I have written this long section on JD Salinger is linked with the reason why I now talk about the life force of sensitivity. Wes, who has helped me to feel okay about having the rich kid blues was himself sparked – in an abstract way – by Salinger. This was crystallised in January 2010, two days after Salinger died, aged 91, from natural causes, when the following short piece by Wes appeared in *The New Yorker*:

> '*I remember this passage from the F Scott Fitzgerald story* The Freshest Boy:
>
> "*He had contributed to the events by which another boy was saved from the army of the bitter, the selfish, the neurasthenic and the unhappy. It isn't given to us to know those rare moments when people are wide open and the lightest touch can wither or heal. A moment too late and we can never reach them any more in this world. They will not be cured by our most efficacious drugs or slain with our sharpest swords.*"
>
> *And it occurred to me that, more than anything else – more than all the things in his stories that I have been inspired by and imitated and stolen to the best of my abilities – THIS described my experience of the works of J D Salinger.*'

WES
THE
ADVENTURER

IN THIS CHAPTER ...

– The sidelined wills of domestic characters

– Turning foreign lands into familiar settings

– Bringing authenticity to fantasy and vice versa

– Running away to Moonrise Kingdom

The low-key trampling of the home-bodies' will

Case study: Mrs Fox

Homebodies tend to be supporting characters in the world of Wes. Adventures blow in and are analysed, but the homebodies do not have a say in the form these adventures take. A best-case scenario is that it enables these characters to look after others. A bonus, sure, but a selfless bonus. Take Mrs Fox, a character born from the wild imagination of Roald Dahl, voiced by the three-time Oscar winner Meryl Streep. This talent combination sounds exciting, especially with Wes in the mix. And yet ...

'If we're still alive tomorrow morning I want you to find another line of work', says Mrs Fox in the opening scene of *Fantastic Mr Fox*. It's two years (12 fox-years) before the main drama is set. To the buccaneering pop beats of 'Heroes and Villains' by The Beach Boys, these vulpine lovers use animal agility to break into Berk's Squab Farm. She is dressed like a hippy, with a bandana and a caftan. She is also pregnant – a fact she reveals after her recklessly curious beau pulls on a chain leading them to be trapped behind bars. At this point she makes her announcement that a career change is in order.

Returning to the present day timeline of the film, Mrs Fox occupies a more classically domestic role. Witness her yellow housedress with its apple pattern, adorned with three pockets from which protrude scissors, a paintbrush and other practical knick-knacks. She approaches her husband, who is buried in a Berliner-style newspaper, holding a cafetiere, like a good Hausfrau. She eases his ego (he is fretting that no one reads his column, 'Fox about town with Mr. Fox') while hustling their cub, Ash, off to school while he feigns sickness.

She may be the droll voice of reason, but his will is what drives the plot and the direction of family life. He decides that they need to move above ground, so they move above ground. He resumes his poaching ways, lying to her and roping in his nephew Kristofferson. This betrayal invites little in the way of domestic consequence. She lashes out once this scheme is exposed, and everything and everyone she knows is threatened by violent death, but hey, he's the fantastic Mr Fox, voiced by the charming George Clooney, and so forgiveness is inevitable.

Meanwhile, her role is vital in that thankless, low-key way that a woman's work has always been vital. She tends to her husband's sore rear after his tail is shot off and keeps a lid on Ash's jealous tantrums. Aside from these nods to her importance, there's simply no space within the narrative, or the family dynamic, for her to do anything but react to that which the men bring into her burrow.

'Oh Foxy, why did you do this to us?' she laments, at one point with their son and nephew awol on a daring expedition.

His answer, that he's a wild animal, is accepted. She adds: 'I should never have married you.'

Living away from home and turning foreign lands into familiar settings

Wes is not a guy who needs to worry about being stuck at home. Following the European travel he did after the release of *The Royal Tenenbaums* in 2003, he wasn't spending more than six months of the year in America. He has kept an apartment in Paris since 2005. His girlfriend, the Lebanese artist Juman Malouf, has a house in Kent. This itinerant lifestyle is reflected in the films that were made after *Tenenbaums*, of which only 2012's *Moonrise Kingdom* was filmed in his home country.

The Life Aquatic was based out of Cinecittà film studios in Rome. *The Darjeeling Limited* involved train-travelling around India, first as it was written, then as it was filmed. *Fantastic Mr Fox* used an English post-production house and deep reconnaissances to Gipsy House in Buckinghamshire. *The Grand Budapest Hotel* was shot in Görlitz on the German-Polish border. *Isle of Dogs* is set in a future Japan but shot in England. In the same way that Wes's hero Louis Malle called his 1969 television series about India, *Phantom India*, to acknowledge the elusiveness of the country's identity to a foreigner, Wes doesn't

posture as a worldly authority on the locations he chooses. He gives us Phantom Italy, Phantom England, Phantom India (the sequel!), Phantom Poland and Phantom Japan. Even films set on home soil seem like Phantom America. Inasmuch as he likes to switch up his cultural backdrops, Wes likes to hang onto his signature wherever in the world he is and by doing so shamelessly flags that he makes cultural fictions, not cultural facts.

The final visions are infused with local spice but their deepest flavour was made in Texas. To critics, his films are repetitive and appropriative. To his fans, they are another instalment in a thematically-linked running series of expressionistic fantasies. No one could ever dub Wes Anderson a lazy man and the details he lifts from other cultures are well-researched and rendered. He has a graphic illustrator's magnetism towards the aesthetic principles of different locales. In *Isle of Dogs* he is interested in marrying ancient aspects of Japanese culture (the ominous taiko drums of war, the haiku as a poetic form, Shōji doors, sushi) with high-tech metal-monster future detailing, and a non-culturally specific Trash Island. And yet the moment a fearsome bedraggled dog named Rex opens his mouth and we hear Ed Norton's reasonable tone, we are in a Wes Anderson movie. (The explanation for using American actors is that the dogs speak a special dog language that has been translated for our ears.) The familiar voices, the symmetrical composition, the 12-year-old boy, the framing devices, all pool under the skin of what is otherwise a radical departure for Wes in setting *and* genre (it's a political conspiracy movie). It creates a sense of home away from home.

As with his lead characters, Wes is a man in motion, but unlike the majority of them – who end up coming back home – he has settled someplace new. In interviews he compares living in Paris to living on a movie set: 'What I like is, if I walk down a street in Paris that I haven't been on before, it's an adventure. Every day that you're abroad, you're discovering something new. When that becomes your routine, it's a strange and interesting way to live.' It makes sense that a man who salutes French directors as his heroes would make their world his own.

Bringing authenticity to fantasies and fantasy to the authentic

On the one hand he has a mania for shooting on location, and will dedicate months to scouting for and deliberating over the perfect place to film. Even in the case of the stop-motion *Fantastic Mr Fox* he had actors record their dialogue on location on a farm in Connecticut – the internet yields footage of George Clooney yelling into the back of a horse trailer. On the other hand, he likes to use visual techniques which hark back to the old Hollywood style of romantic artifice. US writer Scott Eyman was not talking about Wes when he wrote: 'Lubitsch's movies take place neither in Europe nor America but in Lubitschland,' but the point is transferable. Wes has cited a scene in Max Ophuls' 1948 film *Letter From An Unknown Woman* in which Joan Fontaine and Louis Jourdan sit on a train that appears to be real but soon turns out to be a fairground attraction. When Jourdan shouts out

a location, e.g. 'Switzerland' an operator winds an image of The Alps into the window of the train.

The Grand Budapest Hotel is the movie for which Wes most embraced this marriage between physical verisimilitude and snowglobe fantasia. While interiors of the hotel were filmed in a department store, the pink exterior was a 9-foot tall model. Headed up by production designer, Adam Stockhausen, the production team created the backdrop to the hotel by painting a mural of a spa town inspired by the enchanting misty style of Caspar David Friedrich, the 19th-century German Romantic landscape painter. Talking to Terry Gross on NPR in 2014, Wes explained the appeal of literal worldbuilding as twofold: 'There's a certain charm in miniatures to me, I just like them. But also, when you're doing a miniature it means you can make the thing exactly the way you want. You have essentially no limitation.'

The overall effect is to shroud events with a picture-book magic. In this setting characters have the aura of lifesize humans striding through a child's pop-up book, like the best scene in Paul King's *Paddington 2*, or actors that have climbed down from the cinema screen, as in Woody Allen's *The Purple Rose of Cairo*.

Running away to a Moonrise Kingdom

What they leave behind

When they go on the lam together, Sam and Suzy leave behind an imperfect domestic situation in the hope of a life driven by their distinctive interests, and the occasional romantic interlude. He leaves behind a camp of boys and a foster family who – unbeknownst to him – are going to have to let him go. She leaves behind a family home whose comfortable trappings belie a rift between her cheating mother and bellicose father. Suzy is on to all of this, thanks to her dexterous deployment of binoculars (an accessory lifted from the Satyajit Ray film, *Charulata*) through which she observes secret trysts. She has so little use for her mother, father or brothers ('Lionel's a snitch') that her passionate disavowal of her origins leads to this sombre exchange:

Suzy: 'I always wished I was an orphan. Most of my favourite characters are. I think your lives are more special.'

Sam: 'I love you but you don't know what you're talking about.'

What was arrived at

What are these kids able to build together, before the police arrive and Bill Murray lifts up their tent exposing them quivering and holding each other?

How much of it is a sincere expression of lovers liberating their passions, as opposed to scenes constructed to milk the comedy of 12-year-olds acting like Romeo and Juliet? (Although Juliet *was* only 14.)

In the iconic scene where they dance to Françoise Hardy in their underwear on the beach – a scene that came to Wes before he wrote the film – does it *mean* anything, or just look cool?

The answer to these questions lies in the final shot of the film. When Sam tells Suzy that they are at a place called Mile 3.25 Tidal Inlet she frowns and decides a rebrand is in order. 'I need time to think ...' Only at the film's close do we learn the results of her thoughts. Spelled out in rocks on the now empty inlet are the words MOONRISE KINGDOM, like the initials of two lovers etched into the tree trunk. Unlike initials on a tree, this is more than territorial pissing, it is a personal fantasy made real, a title born in the midst of romance. 'There are all kinds of love in the world', wrote F Scott Fitzgerald in his short story collection *Magnetism*, 'but never the same love twice.' What makes a love story more than a mere going through the motions is a unique internal logic, born out of a harmony between two logics. Suzy is a girl who lives through books, Sam is a boy who has made scouting his art. In pursuing their individual interests and allowing them to overlap, they arrive at the creation of Moonrise Kingdom.

CHAPTER
EIGHT

WES
THE
MORTAL

IN THIS CHAPTER ...

- The colourful significance of death
- The characterful significance of death
- Accidents in water
- The suicidal element

A dash of a dark pigment that sets off a bright child's imagination

Early in *The Grand Budapest Hotel* in the wake of the death of the rich Madame D, her sinister, black-clad relatives consult the executor of her estate, Deputy Kovacs. During this meeting, fatal harm is visited upon his cat. Once it becomes clear that the lawyer won't bend to their corrupt requests, his feline is hurled out of a window. Wes's customary bird's eye view shot reveals it spreadeagled and dead. Later Kovacs collects it in a bag, only to bin the bag with comic callousness.

Dismayed by this sequence, Eileen Jones writing in 2015 for *The Jacobin*, expressed the view that violence has no gravitas in Wes's world. In a thoughtful article, she accuses him of using his talents immorally, saying, 'He candy coats a world of casual nastiness in bright colours and hummable tunes.' Advancing the popular theory that Wes is a style over substance guy, she adds that: 'Death in his films makes no mark, it just functions as a design element, a dash of dark pigment that sets off the bright colours to better advantage.'

There is passion and thought behind this critique, and yet I must spring to Wes's defence, like a cat navigating a path away from an ill-wisher. Anderson is a man whose creative imagination was sparked in childhood, at an age when disaster carried as much spectacle as it did horror. This is a quality that Wes has brought into adulthood. It is not born of nastiness, more a light-hearted taste for absurdity. Relish for grotesquerie is thoughtfully blended into the overall tone. He knows and communicates that life is full of tragedy, but rather than hammering this home at every opportunity, he likes to mix it up with schoolboy punchlines to create a colourful palette.

Which isn't to say that he is blasé about violence. Inspired by Robert Altman's 1970 film *M*A*S*H*, about a medical field unit during the Korean war, Wes makes bloody moments bloody, so as to show their severity. Although, to say that he treats death as a dash of dark pigment is only an insult if you don't take pigmentation seriously. And Wes respects aesthetics to death.

Saluting the meaning of loss without succumbing to heavy grief

Death is rarely used to alter the mood of an entire film. Most often it is used to press the plot along or add to the emotional landscape of a character. Wes doesn't make movies that conjure grief. The signature beat of mourning is not synced to movies which unfold at a certain clip. Wes is not a slow cinema guy. Grief is a cloying substance that would see you sleepwalking through a twilight zone for the rest of your god-given life.

Wes may not focus on the bloated emotions that follow in the wake of a meaningful death, but he feeds an understanding of the weight of loss into the worlds that he builds. Mostly he uses death as a way to embellish his characters. One of Max Fisher's most telling lines is when he says to the object of his affection, Miss Cross, 'We both have dead people in our families'. His mum died of cancer, her husband died in a boating accident and he is

harnessing this common ground in an astonishing, brilliant and transparently calculated attempt to cultivate intimacy. Only a very particular type of person could find a tactical use for bereavement, and Max is nothing if not particular.

Physical objects and the earthly mementos left by departed loved ones are markers of absence. Max's mum, Eloise Fisher, left him a typewriter, inscribed with the words, 'Bravo Max! Love Mom'. He uses it to write his plays. Miss Cross's husband, Edward Appleby, left her a book by Jacques Cousteau – *Diving For Sunken Treasure*. She donates it to the Rushmore library, and this is how

Max initially connects with her. Eloise and Edward, though dead, exert their personalities through items that are more revealing than the classic movie method of faded photographs or flashbacks.

The exceptional spiritual bonding in the wake of watery graves

Three deaths take place on screen across Wes's nine feature films. One is fairly peaceful: Royal, a 69-year-old grandfather passing from a heart-attack at the end of *The Royal Tenenbaums* after he has restored good relations with his family. The beep on the heart monitor becomes the continuous sound that signals death as he holds onto the hand of his son, Chas, in the back of an ambulance.

The other two are the untimely accidents of a young man and a young boy: Ned Zissou bleeding to death in the ocean after a helicopter crash in *The Life Aquatic*; and Mukesh Bishnoi being smashed on the rocks after his raft capsizes in *The Darjeeling Limited*.

Of these two, it's *The Darjeeling Limited* that truly weaponises this event, using the death of an unrelated boy to transform the trajectory and closeness of the three Whitman brothers.

We are smack-dab in the middle of the story. Francis, Jack and Peter have been booted off a train for possessing a snake. The three brothers, estranged since their father's death a year previously, had hoped to bond on a spiritual pilgrimage around India which would end with a visit to their elusive mother. All of their aims are looking futile. In addition to having no transport, they have a letter from their mother telling them not to visit. Francis – the oldest and mastermind behind the trip – has a fake tooth which has fallen out. To top it all off, they attempted to be part of a spiritual ceremony the previous evening which went dispiritingly awry.

It is the following morning. Francis is pushing a trolley which holds his suitcases with a laminating machine balanced on top. He is flanked by Peter and Jack who are carrying their luggage. A raging river runs to their right. The laminating machine falls to the ground, crash-zoom into Francis's fed-up and toothless face. He sees something.

Cut to three small Indian boys trying to cross the river using a raft controlled by a rope-pulley which is attached to a tree on one side and a wooden post on the other.

'Look at these assholes.' Francis points at them.
Jack looks. 'That's gonna tip over.'

There is a snap and the raft turns over, flinging its
three small occupants into the air before they land in
the river.

Francis's face. Jack's face. Peter's face.

'Go!' yells Peter.

They run.

Now in the water, they each seem to have one boy
apiece, but Peter says his is 'all tangled up.'

The frame is chaotic for once. Water splashes up
over the lens. Stressful electric sitar music plays. It's
hard to tell exactly what is happening.

'I can't get him out!' Peter is clambering on top of
the capsized raft, then – SNAP – it flips again.

'Peter!' Francis yells.

There is a very emotional edit, resonant of the
Tenenbaums reacting to Richie's suicide attempt,
of Jack running full-pelt alongside the river. Apart
from a heartbeat, the sound is muted, like it is muted
in The Life Aquatic when Steve swims towards his
son, Ned.

Jack shouts as he runs, 'He's all bloody!'

Blood covers the right side of Peter's face, neck
and chest. He is carrying the limp body of the boy in
his arms, like how Steve carries the limp body of Ned.

'He's dead, he's dead,' says Peter in a stunned voice. Adrien Brody's hazel eyes stare in that piercing wounded way. His voice wobbles as he adds, 'The rocks killed him.'

Jack: 'You're bleeding like crazy.'

Francis runs over. 'Peter are you okay?'

'I didn't save mine.' says Peter, then gazing at a living boy. "What's his name?"

This scene is over so quickly. It's 90 seconds of tight drama and, by the end of it, a small boy named Mukesh Bishnoi is dead.

This is an unusual sequence for Wes for a number of reasons. One is that it is played with an entirely straight bat. There is no attempt at humour, just as there is no humour when the Whitman brothers are taken to the village where the boy's father grieves and his body is washed and funeral preparations are made. Two is that it holds the wisdom that each death you experience takes you back to your biggest bereavement. There is a flashback to the brothers en route to their father's funeral and we see what happened the last time they were together. Three is that nothing is the same in the story afterwards. The trio finally have the shared understanding that they couldn't reach beforehand.

The Life Aquatic has two parallel deaths. Shortly after Ned's funeral ends with his casket being cast into the ocean, Team Zissou squish into a submarine to reckon with the Jaguar Shark who killed crew member Esteban. The look on Steve's face during this reckoning (in which he marvels at the beauty of the shark rather than exacting vengeance on it) is one of gawping astonishment. The brash bravado is no more. Instead of performing the role of adventurer he has grown into one, at a cost. Just as the brothers who started *Darjeeling*, by going through the motions of a spiritual journey, end up on a real one as soon as they share a deathly experience. The logic at work here is that there are no routes to true integrated humanity that do not involve accepting and shouldering the pain of death.

For many men there is so much grief

Suicide runs through Wes's films in subtle yet heartfelt ways. The urge for death – for the quieting of the painful world – throbs in the veins of his influences, and finds a body in the performances of Bill Murray whose characters seem to be in the

grip of Thanatos. (According to Freud we are either driven by Eros, the love drive, or Thanatos, the death drive.)

Stefan Zweig, a key literary inspiration for *The Grand Budapest Hotel*, killed himself from a barbiturate overdose in 1942. He was 60, and living in Brazil as a Jewish exile from Austria. His second wife, Charlotte Elisabeth Altmann, overdosed with him. His life and death are chronicled in the dramatised 2016 film, *Stefan Zweig: Farewell to Europe*, directed by Maria Schrader. 'Suicide always remains a secret – the unknown bit beyond all reasons and explanations', said Schrader in a 2017 interview with the *Guardian*. Zweig left a suicide note in which he expresses a desire to bow out at the peak of his cultural powers, and binds his personal fate to the destruction of Europe, in the grip of Nazism at the time of his death. 'I thus prefer to end my life at the right time, upright, as a man for whom cultural work has always been his purest happiness and personal freedom', he wrote.

There is a danger inherent in covering the suicides of cultural figures, a risk of conflating celebration-worthy work with the logic of their final decision. Mystique is seductive, and there are none more mysterious than those who choose death. From a storytelling point of view, suicide is a dramatic flourish, a way of slamming a character's desperation, and it is never exactly clear (not in movies, nor in real life) whether death is intended, as opposed to a cry for help, or the desire for respite from intolerable voices in the head. In writing about people whose deaths are ambiguous, it feels important to tread carefully.

But first: the bleakest of lists – a stock-taking on how suicide touches Wes's work. *The Royal Tenenbaums* has a character who slashes his wrists and a soundtrack which contains tracks by Nick

Drake, whose death from an overdose at 26 was ruled a suicide, and Elliot Smith, whose death from stab wounds at 34 was deemed of inconclusive origin, despite the presence of a possible suicide note. In *Isle of Dogs* there is the tale of Buster, who hung himself using his own leash. Two of Wes's sacred texts have characters who kill themselves. Alain in Louis Malle's *The Fire Within* pulls the trigger of a gun to signal his and the film's end. Seymour Glass shoots himself at the end of JD Salinger's 'A Perfect Day For Bananafish'.

Actual suicides are less evident in Wes's work than a passive death wish glowing within certain characters, especially those played by Bill Murray. As Wes says, 'He has this melancholy side to his screen personality. There's a lot of sadness that just emanates from him, even though he's so funny.' Whether as Raleigh St Clair, a professor in a velvet jacket and bottle glasses, saying, 'Well I want to die' before taking a bite of biscuit; whether as Steve Zissou remaining where he has fallen at the bottom of the stairs; whether as Walt lying in bed wishing to be sucked up into the sky in *Moonrise Kingdom*; he expresses despair as a feeling buried so deep that it manifests as physical stillness and a tortured, middle-distance stare.

Rushmore contains a sequence that illustrates his state of mind perfectly. Herman Blume, 'the tycoon' (to call him by the film's original title) is at a pool party for his twin sons with whom he has a fractious relationship. They open presents, while Herman sits alone at a table, expressionless, smoking, and throwing golf balls into the green water of the pool. The caressing strums of 'Nothing in this World' by The Kinks kick in. Herman turns to look across the pool. A woman is flirtatiously forking cake into a man's mouth. She senses Herman's gaze and her coquettish expression drops. A brief flashback to a family portrait (also shown in the opening credits) reveals this woman to be Herman's wife.

A tiny blond boy in red swimming trunks swings by Herman's table to pick up a piece of cake. Herman keeps throwing golf balls into the pool. Then he walks to the diving board, a tumbler of whisky in one hand, and a cigarette in the other. Ray Davies is singing in a cloyingly sweet voice about being two-timed. Herman climbs the diving board ladder to its very top. He chugs his whisky and looks down at the pool party guests watching him from below. (On the Criterion commentary, Owen Wilson says this is a 'How did I get here?'

moment referencing the Talking Heads song 'Once in a Lifetime'.)

Herman takes a run up and, indifferent to the assembled crowd below, canon-balls into the pool. A huge plume of water results from his descent. Now that he's below the surface, everything is calm. Herman holds himself down in a foetal position, seeming to find peace in this subterranean cocoon. And this is what conveys the feeling of drowning in your life, being present and absent at the same time. The tender music aligns with the tenderness buried within the bulk of Bill Murray. The seductive treacle of despair seeps into the frame.

The thing about seeing despair rendered on screen is that, conversely, it offers hope. If you ever felt a crushing sense of life's impossibility then seeing that state given full-guns-blazing cinema treatment reminds you that you're still connected to humanity, because art is made by humans. When an artist takes a risk by rendering dangerous levels of vulnerability, it's a gesture which has potential to stir anyone who looks to cinema for solace. 'What I love about movies is the feeling that somebody made them. What makes me want to see a film is the feeling that I'm meeting someone. Who is on the other side of this film? Who is talking to me?'

said the French director Mia Hansen-Løve to *Little White Lies* magazine in 2014, crystallising the way that art is a personal offering.

Often the bleakest emotions are too intense to accept and people cut off from them, which only aggravates the feeling of being disconnected. The paradox channeled by Bill Murray and Wes Anderson is that numb characters are used to convey deep sensitivity. Once you are dead you will feel nothing. If you want to live you must feel everything, even depression. Wes, in his consistent rendering of acute melancholia, encourages the crumbling of the walls within.

EPILOGUE

'I do believe if you don't like things you leave for some place you've never been before.'

This is a line from 'I Found The Reason' by The Velvet Underground. It is not a song Wes has used in a film, but it's linked to his sensitivities by virtue of being '60s/'70s rock 'n' roll. And, to go full nerd, a different Velvet Underground track, 'Stephanie Says' scores a father/son bonding scene in *The Royal Tenenbaums*.

Anyway, this lyric is freeing. It evokes the idea of an adventurer and the open road. But what if you are the one who is left behind? Or what if you do like things and still have to leave? Like the mother who abandoned the Whitman brothers. "Yes the past happened, but it's over, isn't it?" she tells her boys when they finally locate her in a nunnery. "Not for us," retorts Francis.

Where there is a difference between the levels of attachment people hold for each other there is separation pain. There is a vast difference between the attachment I feel to Wes Anderson – a living filmmaker whose work I cherish – and the attachment he feels to me – a person whose existence he has barely registered. The relationship between an art fan and the artist is the most humbling type of unrequited love. Not only is your love unreturned, but you are expressing it into empty space, or vomiting fragments of it into the ears of friends, or parsing it into a book... that you will eventually have to finish.

'Can you separate art from the artist?' is a common question, usually asked in connection with men who have done terrible things. On the flip side: when you love a work of art, do you also love the artist? And is that love a true read on the work, or a projection of a desirous imagination? The French writer Stendhal described a concept of 'crystallisation' in relation to love: 'The moment one begins to take interest in a person, one no longer sees him or her as they really are, but as it suits one to see them.'

By serendipity I came to interview Wes Anderson, not for this book, but for an issue of *Little White Lies* featuring *Isle of Dogs*. The process of nailing down a time and place was tortuous. In early January of 2018 it was suggested that I would interview him in person at a cat cafe in Paris. That soon shifted to London. There was a brief notion that I would interview him over email, then it became clear that it would be over the phone. New information came to light that Wes wanted to do the interview with his co-writers Jason Schwartzman and Roman Coppola, so it looked like a four-way conference call was in the offing. But then – hallelujah! – that was a timezone snafu.

At 3 p.m. GMT on Tuesday 13 February, as Wes passed through Switzerland on a train from Paris bound for Berlin, we spoke for 30 minutes broken up by a single disconnection as he went under a tunnel.

Woven into my list of questions were prompts into the territory I was dying to explore: the emotional frequency of his movies and the melancholy, mined over the course of this book, that has so moved me. When the conversation went in the right direction I dropped my bombs and waited for the explosions. Instead we rolled onwards amiably, as he shot through Europe on a train and I lay on my bed wondering how to alchemise all my research into questions that would take us to the next level. An anti-climax was inevitable. Everything I asked was met with a thoughtful, honest, helpful answer that scanned well in the lead interview spot, and still ... all I felt was the unbreachable distance between us.

Two days after our interview, *Isle of Dogs* opened the Berlin Film Festival. I watched the full 46-minute press conference on *The Film Stage* website. A long table filled up with Jason Schwartzman, Roman

Coppola, Greta Gerwig, Bob Balaban, Bill Murray, Bryan Cranston, Wes, Koyu Rankin, Liev Schreiber, Jeff Goldblum and Konichu Nomura. The film family were on peak form. Every time a question was directed at Bob Balaban, Bill Murray led a song about his name to the tune of 'Barbara Ann' by The Beach Boys. Wes was glowing, making jokes all over the place, sitting snugly in the middle of these people who drummed up this magical feeling of being collaborative dreamweavers.

Sitting at home I felt love, admiration, envy and loneliness. I wanted to be more than a detached bystander chronicling Wes from afar. Having talked while he was on a train created an impression of flying through space, creating a momentum which remained. It was so intimate for a moment. It was like being in a private cocoon, but it was over so quickly, and now he had moved on and was addressing a room full of journalists in Berlin.

I began this book by talking about the recurring theme of families – the agony and ecstasy of our closest bonds. There is a psychological theory that we need closeness to experience intimacy but separation to experience desire. Wes works with a lot of the same people, but they are not constantly part of his life, when he sees them on film sets it marks a reunion of sorts. He is not immune to the dance of coming closer and then moving away from loved ones that is part of harbouring independent ambitions. When someone elicits a strong feeling, the impulse in you is to feel great sorrow as you sense a goodbye coming. And yet ...

As the German poet Rainer Maria Rilke wrote: 'Once the realisation is accepted that even between the closest human beings infinite distances continue, a wonderful living side by side can grow, if they succeed in loving the distance which makes it possible to see the other whole against the sky.'

Whether real or imagined, the Phantom Wes I have spiritually communed with night after night in the conceiving and writing of this book feels like family. I will miss spending time with him. However to be truly inspired by him means making like the Whitman brothers at the end of *The Darjeeling Limited*, and throwing away baggage in order to move forwards, content that whatever is important enough to have been internalised will guide me from within. As Anjelica Huston says, in her last words of the film, 'To be continued ...'

FURTHER READINGS, VIEWINGS AND RESEARCH

Bottle Rocket

1. *Ravel's String Quartet in F Major by the Britten Quartet*

2. *Mean Streets* (Martin Scorsese, 1973)

3. *The 400 Blows* (François Truffaut, 1959)

Rushmore

1. *A Charlie Brown Christmas* (Bill Melendez, 1965)

2. *The Graduate* (Mike Nichols, 1967)

3. *Harold and Maude, Hal Ashby* (1971) For the plot and the music by Cat Stevens.

The Royal Tenenbaums

1. *The Magnificent Ambersons* (Orson Welles, 1942)

2. JD Salinger's Glass family stories, *Franny and Zooey* and *Nine Stories.*

3. *Le Feu Follet* (Louis Malle, 1963)

4. *It's the Great Pumpkin, Charlie Brown* (Bill Melendez, 1966)

5. *Two English Girls* (François Truffaut, 1971) For the book-patterned title cards.

The Life Aquatic with Steve Zissou

1. Richard Avedon's photographs of Italian twins in the '60s.

2. Fashion photographs of Anjelica Huston.

3. *Playtime* (Jacques Tati, 1967)

4. *Tokyo Story* (Yasukiro Ozu, 1953)

5. *The Silent World* (Jacques Cousteau, Louis Malle, 1956)

The Darjeeling Limited

1. *The River* (Jean Renoir, 1951)

2. *Phantom India* (Louis Malle, 1966)

3. Films by Satyajit Ray: *Pather Panchali* (1955); *Teen Kanya* (1961); *Abhijan* (1962); *Charulata* (1964)

4. *Lola* (Jacques Demy, 1961)

Fantastic Mr Fox

1. *Michael Clayton* (Tony Gilroy, 2007) For George Clooney's performance.

2. The literary corpus of Roald Dahl.

3. *The Tale of the Fox* (Ladislas Starevich, 1930)

4. Stop-motion animator Ray Harryhausen - for example *Jason and the Argonauts* (1963).

5. *My Fair Lady* (George Cukor, 1964) Mr Fox was modelled to look like Rex Harrison and Roald Dahl.

6. *King Kong* (Merian C. Cooper and Ernest B. Shoedsack, 1933) For Willis O'Brien's animation style.

Moonrise Kingdom

1. *Charulata* (Satyajit Ray, 1964) For the binoculars.

2. *Play: Our Town* (Thornton Wilder) Inspired Bob Balaban's narrator.

3. *Badlands* (Terrence Malick, 1973) For the plot and racoon eyes.

4. *Black Jack* (Ken Loach, 1979)

5. *Melody* (Waris Hussein, 1971)

6. *Small Change* (François Truffaut, 1976)

The Grand Budapest Hotel

1. *The Red Shoes* (Michael Powell and Emeric Pressburger, 1948) Adrien Brody is dressed as Lermentov.

2. The writings of Stefan Zweig, especially *Beware of Pity*, but also *The Post Office Girl* and *The World of Yesterday*.

3. *Heart of Glass* (Werner Herzog, 1976) Inspired the yodelling.

4. *Letter from an Unknown Woman* (Max Ophuls, 1948)

5. *Raising Arizona* (The Coen brothers, 1987)

6. *Dune* (David Lynch, 1984) For the invented politics.

7. Paintings by Caspar David Friedrich.

8. Paintings by Gustav Klimt.

9. Paintings by Egon Schiele – A painting used in the film (of two lesbian lovers) is an original, but based on Schiele.

10. Albrecht Dürer's 'Self-Portrait'.

11. Hans Holbein the Younger's 'Portrait of George Giese'.

12. Bronzino's 'Portrait of a Young Man'.

Isle of Dogs

1. The films of Akira Kurosawa, particularly *Dodes'ka-den* (1970), *High and Low* (1963) and *Drunken Angel* (1948).

2. The films of Hayao Miyazaki, particularly *Porco Rosso* (1992).

3. *Snoopy Come Home* (Bill Melandez,1972)

4. *Akira* (Katsuhiro Otomo, 1988)

5. *The Tale of Princess Kaguya* (Isao Takahata, 2014)

6. Rankin Bass Christmas specials.

7. *The Plague Dogs* (Martin Rosen, 1982)

8. *101 Dalmatians* (Wolfgang Reitherman, Clyde Geronimi, Hamilton Luske, 1961)

9. These television shows: *Fat Albert*, *Sanford and Son*, *Sesame Street* – with special mention to Oscar the Grouch.

ACKNOWLEDGMENT FROM THE AUTHOR

This book is for one of the very best of us, David Jenkins.

William Collins
An imprint of HarperCollinsPublishers
1 London Bridge Street
London SE1 9GF

www.WilliamCollinsBooks.com
First published in Great Britain by William Collins in 2018

1

A catalogue record for this book is
available from the British Library.

ISBN 978-0-00-825658-6

Page 91: Extract from 'Fidelity' by Ted Hughes taken from Birthday
Letters (Faber and Faber, 1998); **Page 106**: Extract by Arthur Goldman
taken from Memoirs of a Geisha (Alfred A. Knopf, 1997);
Page 166: Quotation taken from the New Yorker, 'Wes Anderson on
J. D. Salinger'; https://www.newyorker.com/culture/richard-brody
/wes-anderson-on-j-d-salinger

Series editors: David Jenkins, Tom Killingbeck, Clive Wilson
Cover illustration by Christopher DeLorenzo
Interior illustrations by Yann Le Bec
Design and layout: Oliver Stafford, Laurène Boglio, Sophie Mo

Printed and bound by CPI Group (UK) Ltd, Croydon, CR0 4YY